The Economics of Place:

The Art of Building Great Communities

Authored by Elizabeth Philips Foley, Colleen Layton, Daniel Gilmartin:

Elizabeth Philips Foley is a special projects writer for the Michigan Municipal League, and a former newspaper journalist. She is also the co-author of "The Lone Wolverine: Tracking Michigan's Most Elusive Animal" (The University of Michigan Press, 2012).

Colleen Layton is Director of Policy Development at the Michigan Municipal League. She focuses time and effort on leveraging the League's policy goals not only to the League's members, but to other organizations and groups around the state.

Dan Gilmartin is the executive director and chief executive officer of the Michigan Municipal League. Through his work with communities, Dan is recognized as a national leader in the fields of urban revitalization, placemaking, local government reform, and transportation policy.

Edited by Colleen Layton, Tawny Pearson, Lisa Donovan

Thank you to the Michigan Municipal League Board of Trustees for their continuing support.

Published by the Michigan Municipal League
1675 Green Road, Ann Arbor, MI 48105
www.mml.org

Printed by: Printwell, Taylor, Michigan

Book Design by:

genui f o r ma

print design | web media | branding

www.genuiforma.com

Ann Arbor, Michigan

ISBN 978-1-929923-00-7

Table of Contents

Acknowledgements

A special thanks to those who helped to bring this book together

The Economics of Place: The Art of Building Communities illustrates the power of people who believe that they can make a difference in their communities. We feel privileged to have met with them to hear their inspiring stories. With their sharing and support, we were able to learn about some of the great placemaking projects taking place around the state of Michigan. The people we met along the way were gracious and generous with their time, carving out hours from their busy days to share their pride and passion for the places they call home. Their invaluable insights and guidance were an inspiration to all of us.

Although the list is long, we want to recognize the individuals from the communities, organizations, and businesses who embraced this book project and welcomed us with open arms.

Our heartfelt thanks go out to Baroda Village President Bob Getz and Village Clerk Tina Boehm; Greta and Bill Hurst of Tabula Rosa; planning consultant Chuck Eckenstahler; Select Tool and Die, Inc.; Bridgman City Manager Aaron Anthony; the Moersch family of Round Barn Winery Distillery and Brewery; St. Julian Winery; Johnny's Barbershop; Rose's Concrete; and Steve Salisbury of Worthenbury Country House. In addition, many thanks to Paw Paw City Manager Larry Nielsen for his time and assistance in providing data for the case study of "Uncork Paw Paw."

We are grateful for all the work that has been done and for those who continue to advocate for bike trails in Michigan. These include Lake Orion Downtown Development Authority Executive Director Suzanne Perreault and staff member Janet Harman; Oakland Township Parks and Recreation Commissioner Alice Tomboulian; Oakland Township Historic District Commission Historic Preservation Planner Barbara Barber; Ed Granchi of Paint Creek Cider Mill LLC; retired Paint Creek Trailways Commissioner Peggy Johnson and Trail Manager Kristen Myers; Kristy Kowatch of Twice Blessed Children's and Divas Women Consignment; Beth Lofay of Simply Marcella; Lloyd Coe of Ed's Broadway Gifts & Costumes; Community Planner Harry Burkholder of the Land Information Access Association (LIAA); Michigan Trails and Greenways Alliance board member Jack Minore; and the Noquemanon Trail Network.

A special thanks to the people from Wonderfool Productions who invited us in to experience the behind-the-scenes wonderment of puppet making. These include Creative Director and Founder Mark Tucker, Executive Director Shary Brown, and Detroit Thanksgiving Parade Art Director Jimmie Thompson. Thank you also to Francis Grunow for his valuable contributions to our case study on Detroit's Nain Rouge event.

Thank you to our own Sean Mann, a former member of the Michigan Municipal League staff and Detroit City Futbol founder, whose passion for Detroit and "survival stories" were always an inspiration to us. Also, thank you to Tania Bennett Allen, a Detroit City Futbol League member whose enthusiasm is echoed by all members of the soccer teams. For the case study, a thank you to everyone at Detroit Soup who has worked so hard to foster entrepreneurism and community spirit, while inspiring similar projects around the state.

Thank you to the Kalamazoo folks who are leading the way with the power of local food and community engagement: Kalamazoo Mayor Bobby Hopewell and staff; Food Dance owner Julie Stanley and former Executive Chef Robb Hammond; Pat Smith Kirklin of Kirklin Farms; Trent and Ruthie Thompson of Green Gardens Farm; Kalamazoo Farmers' Market Manager Chris Boardbent; Kalamazoo People's Food Co-Op General Manager Chris Dilley; Webster's Prime Executive Chef Stefan Johnson, Kitchen Supervisor Nate Shaw, Event Coordinator Alexa Tipton, and former Sous Chef Jud McMichael; Zazios Executive Chef John Korycki; and Flint Farmers Market Manager Richard Ramsdell and Assistant Manager Karianne Martus for their assistance in preparing the case study.

We are very grateful to Traverse City Film Festival Founder Michael Moore, Executive Director Deb Lake, and Production Director Meg Weichman. Their vision of a film festival has resonated all over the world. Thank you to Traverse City Tourism President & CEO Brad Van Dommelen; Traverse City Manager Jered Ottenwess, DDA Executive Director Rob Bacigalupi; and film festival volunteer Donna Valdmanis. And a big thank you to Ludington resident Bill Anderson who provided information and more for Ludington's case study. He has been a catalyst and enthusiastic booster for public art in his hometown.

Michigan is defined by its beautiful waterfronts. Two waterfront cities that are creating a place that is attracting talent by celebrating their unique assets are Marquette and St. Joseph. We extend our appreciation to Marquette City Manager William Vajda and Marquette County Convention and Visitors Bureau Executive Director Pat Black for their time and knowledge, and Caroline Weber Kennedy, former manager of field operations at the Michigan Municipal League and now executive officer of the Traverse City Home Builders Association. For the case study, we thank the City of St. Joseph Director of Communications/Marketing Susan D. Solon, St. Joseph Today Executive Director Jill Stone, St. Joseph City Manager Richard L. Lewis, Frank L. Walsh, township manager for Charter Township of Meridian, and the entire "Silver Beach Center Team" who made the project possible.

And last but not least—just because the name of their deli begins with a Z—is a huge shout-out to Zingerman's. Many thanks to Cofounder Paul Saginaw and his team of employees whose unfailing commitment helps make this business an integral part of the community. We thank Tom Root, co-founder at Maker Works and owner and managing partner at Zingerman's Mail Order; Lynn Yates, manager of the Community Chest program; Robby Griswold, Community Partnerships coordinator and chair, Diversity and Inclusion Committee; and Charlie Frank, founder and managing partner of Candy Manufactory. And for our food cart case study, we always enjoy a lunch hour at Mark's Carts thanks to the owner of Ann Arbor's Downtown Home and Garden and founder of Mark's Carts, Mark Hodesh. He has created a wonderful, organic space to bring people together.

We hope that we haven't left anyone out, and if we did, our sincere apologies. Just know that this book wouldn't have been possible without all of you who supported us and shared your wisdom in the creation of this book. We are all truly on a journey of building great places in Michigan and hopefully inspiring others along the way.

Creating great places isn't a linear activity. Sustaining them is even trickier.

Introduction by Daniel Gilmartin

Human beings have been in the business of city-making since before recorded history. People would build cities then proceed to destroy, rebuild, sack, abandon, reimagine, and resurrect them. Cities would face war, famine, floods, and disease—always changing and adjusting to meet new challenges. The result was a Darwinian prototype of the city—resilient, connected, and structured, with enough room for a measure of authenticity.

Cities built before World War II usually used the age-old model—a compact street grid programmed for walking and public transportation alike. Cultural and recreational activities were accessible on a neighborhood-by-neighborhood basis. The human experience was a primary focus of this type of community design, whether it was chatting with a neighbor on a short walk to work or window-shopping along storefronts on the way home.

Then along came 1945. I reference that year because it marks the end of WWII, the beginning of the baby boomer generation, and a demarcation point for how we build cities in America. In the decades that followed WWII, the country saw an explosion in population. New government programs wrested Americans away from traditional cities with promises of better lives beyond their borders. The federal government built eight-lane highways in every direction and subsidized mortgages for new construction in green fields. State government policies soon followed suit, forever changing the landscape of the nation and altering the definition of what it meant to be a prosperous community.

For certain, there were valid reasons for attempting something new in the city-building arena. Pollution, overcrowding, and concentration of poverty are historic problems in large cities. Many believed that spreading housing and commercial enterprises over more land would ease these urban ailments.

As we know, these pivotal changes in urban planning did not "fix" the problems in cities. They did create a whole new set of land-use challenges that have yet to be grasped in their entirety.

Ok, I know what you're thinking, "Here comes a lecture on the evils of car-centered cultures and livability." Nope. Not going to happen. The focus of this book is not city design. Instead, I would like to zero in on one important consequence of the new design theories that I believe marks the genesis of the placemaking movement.

That single issue is the connectivity of people.

A dense network of streets and buildings breeds human connection. People have known this for thousands of years, having evolved the concept from small villages to grand cities. We found that compact design and a mix of housing, commercial uses, and open space led to increased livability for everyone. Street life was important. Neighborhoods had their own idiosyncrasies, which fed the larger city's own unique cultural landscape. Center cities acted as the hub of a regional wheel. The established model was both efficient and resilient.

Then…we changed course. Under the banner of civic progress, compact development was replaced by a less dense variety. Out went the walk to work and in came long automobile commutes. Chain stores trumped local merchants. Some of it works, much of it doesn't.

I think it was about this time that the term subdivision began to replace the word neighborhood in the common American lexicon.

One area forever damaged by the shift was

human connection — human beings became much less connected to those around them. Now, in the early years of the 21st century, we are coming to grips with how this dynamic harmed everything from innovation and commerce to cultural identity and quality of life.

Derived from a desire to be better, the placemaking movement aims to create positive change on streets, in neighborhoods, and everywhere.

Why Placemaking?

Placemaking, at its core, is a response. It follows in the long tradition of humanist reactions to systems that come to rely too much on dogma and tradition that runs afoul of everyday life. Federal policy that favors similarity in housing styles, cumbersome city codes that sap entrepreneurial spirit, and a lack of effective civic engagement around decision-making all lead to citizen dissatisfaction. Throw in overbearing planning and zoning laws that often outlaw the types of places that people covet, and you have a pretty potent recipe for backlash.

Placemaking, in a nut shell, is about positioning the human experience in everyday life above all else. People are social creatures. At our best, we like to feel part of a larger plan for our families and our communities. Greeting people on a walkable street or chatting with old friends while enjoying a public space are important components of city life. So are groups of entrepreneurs exchanging ideas at a local coffee shop or a public art show that dots the neighborhood landscape on weekends in the summer. All these events contribute to the vibrancy of the human experience and have positive impacts on culture, health, and the economy.

I cannot stress the importance of a community's unique culture enough. Public art is often the first item on the chopping block during difficult budget times. This follows the pattern set for art classes in public schools. In both cases, doing so is shortsighted and robs communities of their ability to celebrate their own history, as well as learn about faraway places and people.

By comparison, the communities that have placed arts and culture higher on the pecking order have seen real increases in important measures, such as community participation, historic preservation, and the ability to draw foreign investment.

The 80 million members of the millennial generation place a heavy emphasis on arts and culture. Cookie cutter cities that don't offer an array of cultural offerings cannot compete for them. Call it the Anti-Applebee's Effect. A city that has sameness and order as its calling card is not seen as a desirable destination compared to places that offer grit, unique venues, and the dynamism that comes with those who seek out such destinations.

Communities that practice placemaking are also healthy communities. The accessibility of walkable streets, public spaces, and outdoor activities are all important aspects of placemaking. It is a shame that in some places, due to planning decisions at city hall, it makes more sense for people to drive their cars to the gym to walk on a treadmill, rather than take a stroll along the city streets because of speeding automobile traffic, a lack of sidewalks, or improper lighting in the evening. Folks, that's just nuts! We need to do better.

In *The Economics of Place: The Value of Building Communities Around People*, I outlined the connection between great places and economic opportunity. In the three years since the book's publication, the trend towards utilizing placemaking as an economic driver has exploded. We know that people are more mobile today than ever before. We also know they are choosing to locate in cities at a higher rate. Jobs, and in some cases entire industries, are mobile as well. Nowhere has this fact been more pronounced than in my home state of Michigan. The collapse of heavy manufacturing in the final days of the 20th century and the first decade of the 21st put the once prosperous state near the bottom of many dubious lists—job loss, per capita income, and unemployment, to name a few. Our largest city saw population loss at staggering levels. Many predicted more gloom and doom for the Mitten State.

It pleases me to report that something much different happened on the way to the funeral, and the state is seeing real growth for the first time in decades. The successful, and at times painful, restructuring of large scale industry was an important factor in the turnaround. But something else is shaping the future Michigan—recognition that unique places that feature cultural enrichment and a high quality of experience boost economic as well as social conditions. Whether through dogged entrepreneurial determination or special programs and policies, Michigan is at the cutting-edge of utilizing placemaking as a long-term, sustainable economic instrument. Its cities and their people are leading the way.

I have had the pleasure of working with renowned architect and city booster, Andrés Duany, in recent years. One of his tenets for improving underperforming urban places is that they must be open to the risk-oblivious among us, because they are the ones who start the comeback. Maybe they are urban pioneers reshaping buildings and neighborhoods where others have given up. Perhaps it is an entrepreneur who views cheap rent in a bad part of town as an opportunity to set up shop and get to work on their vision of the American Dream. The risk-oblivious also play the important "first-in" role that does the initial dirty work which makes it possible for the risk-tolerant and the risk-adverse to stake their claim. Think of them as the Marines of city-building. Duany warns that cities that block the risk-oblivious in favor of those who fall much further down the scale of hazard tolerance (large developers, traditional banks, and heavy industry) will fail. There are scores of examples of cities that have gambled their futures on a collection of sham silver bullets that led to further decline. Does anybody remember Auto World or the first incarnation of the Renaissance Center?

Besides identifying fresh economic opportunities in downtrodden areas, the risk-oblivious also play a significant role in establishing culture and defining physical space. Later chapters in the book detail how this activity leads to the creation of energy. It is this energy that becomes a catalyst for economically significant placemaking. We're seeing the restoration of historic homes, updates to downtown storefronts, and new opportunities for growth in neighborhoods. The results are unique, resilient places that are fun to be in and are attractive to people, especially the mobile sort who drive today's economy.

Placemaking in Michigan

Perhaps more than any other state, Michigan has grabbed the placemaking agenda and run with it. The confluence of the risk-oblivious and a traditional set of characters tired of the decline have led the way. While it is way too early to declare victory, the trends are heading in the right direction. According to a 2014 University of Michigan survey of elected city leaders, more than one-third of the state's cities have utilized placemaking as a development strategy, an increase of 21 percent since 2009. These survey results prove that local government leaders talk the placemaking talk and walk the placemaking walk. From the Traverse City Film Festival to the Noquemanon Trail Network in the Upper Peninsula to the FestiFools in Ann Arbor, communities are celebrating their uniqueness and beginning to make better use of their own distinctive assets. They are redesigning streets to provide a better balance for bikers and walkers in small towns like West Branch and big cities like Detroit. They are celebrating local culture in Ludington, supporting entrepreneurs in Houghton, and valuing the everyday human experience everywhere. The stories in this book illustrate the power and the promise of placemaking in many of its forms.

The formation of an effective placemaking culture is taking hold. It's common these days to see social entrepreneurs partnering with business people in Detroit, arts activists working with city officials in Grand Rapids, or philanthropic organizations spearheading civic engagement projects. At the state level, the Michigan Municipal League and the Michigan State Housing Development Authority (MSHDA) have provided leadership to the Sense of Place Council, which includes members from the state's top organizations representing small business, the environment, community development agencies, and more. Representatives from affected state departments are also part of the discussion. The creation of the council in 2010 was "in response to the economic and social challenge facing Michigan—a transition from an industrial, manufacturing-based economy to a diversified 'place-based' economy embracing talent, entrepreneurship, creativity, and innovation." Acting as a kind of sounding board for place-based thinking, the council plays a key role in connecting the different players together to advocate for changes in state policy, and to provide help to local efforts. It's a regular gathering of the innovators within the grand placemaking laboratory that is Michigan.

What's Next?

As I see it, there are three major goals for the future of placemaking. The first goal is to do more of what is working. We must continue to innovate around the creation of great places. There are scores of important placemaking experiments taking place inside the Great Lakes State. These tests are important to improving places everywhere.

It is also paramount that we discover new ways to scale the achievements. This one is a bit tricky because great placemaking is often organic and not meant to extend to an entire community or act as a model for others. I see this as a challenge in cities like Detroit, where certain areas have seen enormous progress in recent years, but there remain large swaths of blight. We are finding, as others before us, that attempting to optimize innovative practices is wrought with difficulty. Still, we need to find a way.

This brings us to the act of governance. Technology aside, the basic governing models used by municipalities in the 1950s remain in place today. It is time that we change. The lack of evolution led noted urban champion Christopher Leinberger to state, "Expecting early 19th century or even mid-20th century governance structures to handle the challenges of the early 21st century is not realistic."

From my perspective, creating and sustaining new governing structures around 'place' is the Holy Grail of the movement. Our work has shown that when you move key decision-making out of city hall and place it in the hands of citizens and neighborhood groups, the results are terrific. Thriving cities like Portland and Seattle have made excellent use of the practice. Struggling places need to adapt as well. Detroit is beginning this journey. Their financial troubles, which led to a 2013 municipal bankruptcy filing, created a colossal hole in the city's service delivery. Parks closed, emergency response times increased to absurd levels, and the municipal government ceased many services deemed basic in other communities. If there is a silver lining, it is that this crisis is leading to innovative practices that would not have happened otherwise. A lack of city inspectors for blighted properties birthed strategies that involve neighborhood groups in the nuisance abatement process, which is something they had wanted to do for years. Smaller community groups have taken responsibility for public parks, arts programming, and even commercial property redevelopment. Businesses have stepped up by programming public spaces, and philanthropy is ever-present in pushing the agenda forward.

New leadership in city hall is beginning to embrace a modern role as a convener and a catalyst for local innovators, while concentrating limited resources on the necessities for quality of life. At the League, we often tell government leaders to be the host of the party, not the life of it. This advice is good for all cities, not just for those who are struggling, and it provides the perfect metaphor for policies that make places great.

The stories that you will read in this book provide models of what can happen when we place the human experience atop the city-building pyramid. There are examples of great programs; lists of things to consider in your own hometown when confronting similar challenges; and recognition for those who have shown great leadership. You'll view the results of a Hollywood filmmaker's quest to revive old theaters and see how one company is walking the line between preserving their own values on sustainability and making a profit. Along the way, we'll highlight some great public spaces, cultural offerings, and new community designs that are positioning our state to capitalize on our distinctive assets. It is a source of great pride that our collective work continues to inspire cities across the globe and provide direction for significant bodies like the National League of Cities and the United Nations. My hope is that this book provides you with encouragement and a practical set of tools for making your corner of the world more enjoyable for everyone who touches it.

DANIEL GILMARTIN *serves as the executive director and CEO of the Michigan Municipal League, the state's association of communities formed in 1899.*

Daniel P. Gilmartin

Agritourism can mean many things: dude ranch resorts, rural bed-and-breakfast tours, volunteer vacations on organic farms, pick-your-own orchards, and everything in between. What they share in common is a sense of place built on a region's farming heritage. It connects our largely urban/suburban society back to its agricultural roots while helping to protect farming as a sustainable way of life. The end result is placemaking at its most natural and fundamental level.

Kiva Bottero, editor of The Mindful Word journal of engaged living (themindfulword.org) and Green Building Canada (greenbuildingcanada. ca) had this to say about the two poles of that synergistic relationship: "Farming is an incredibly unstable business, subject to the whims of Mother Nature. Even as food prices rise, farmers rarely benefit. Opening up to tourism is a way for them to diversify their operation and make money even in the worst of droughts… Conversely, more than half the world's population lives in cities. The skills required to be self-sufficient are quickly becoming lost with each successive generation. Even just a few days on a farm can reconnect anyone, from the truly city slick to the agri-curious, to our traditional way of life—lifetimes of tradition that are well worth experiencing, learning, and passing along to future generations."[1]

In several states, including Michigan, viticulture is one of the fastest growing parts of the agricultural industry, and wine country agritourism has become one of the most successful trends in regional placemaking. According to the National Grape & Wine Initiative (NGWI), 14 U.S. states produced 7,343,405 tons of grapes on 962,100 acres in 2012, yielding $4,911,335,000 of production value.[2] Of that, 4.4 million tons were wine grapes. The placemaking significance of that goes far beyond product sales.

Here are a few stats from a 2007 economic impact study by MKF Research LLC of Napa Valley, unveiled on Capitol Hill by the Congressional Wine Caucus:[3]

- Wine Industry Direct Impact: 4,929 wineries in 2005, up from 2,904 in 2000, a 70 percent increase in 5 years; wineries now in all 50 states; $11.4 billion in winery sales revenues.
- Wine Industry Value Added: $2.7 billion in distributor share of American wine revenue; $9.8 billion in retail and restaurant share of American wine revenue; 27.3 million wine-related tourist visits; $3 billion estimated wine-related tourism expenditures.

AGRITOURISM

• Other Grape Products: $1.669 billion retail value of grape juice and grape product sales; $3 billion retail value of table grape sales; $560 million retail value of raisin sales.

• Total Taxes Paid: $17.1 billion, including $9.1 billion federal and $8 billion state and local.

According to the NGWI: "Wine in particular has an enormous value-added component as a capital-intensive and labor-intensive industry which also generates 'wine country' tourism with its economic multiplier effect around the country. The infrastructure, employees, and tourism expenditures are just three examples of why wine sales are only part of the picture in terms of total economic impact."[4]

(ENDNOTES)

1 Kiva Bottero, "Agritourism: Reconnect to an Agricultural Way of Life," Sustainable Cities Collective (blog), May 27, 2013, accessed March 12, 2014, http://sustainablecitiescollective.com/bigvibes/153616/agritourism-relax-and-reconnect-agricultural-way-life.

2 National Grape & Wine Initiative, "U.S. Grape Industry Stats," January 2013 Summary, accessed March 12, 2014.http://www.ngwi.org/us-grape-industry-stats_220.html.

3 MKF Research LLC, "The Impact of Wine, Grapes, and Grape Products on the American Economy 2007: Family Businesses Building Value," accessed March 12, 2014, http://www.ngwi.org/files/documents/Economic_Impact_on_National_Economy_2007.pdf.

4 National Grape & Wine Initiative, "Economic Impact Study," January 17, 2007, accessed March 12, 2014, http://www.ngwi.org/economic-impact-study_226.html.

from great lake to great grapes

Agritourism in Lake Michigan
Shore Wine Country

It's wine touring season in southwest Michigan. Far across the water, where Lake Michigan's shoreline curves down against Indiana, the hazy outline of factories and smokestacks edges the horizon, marking the industrial region at Chicago's southern doorstep. But all along the Red Arrow Highway on the Michigan side, a steady stream of travelers makes their way up the sandy coastline from New Buffalo to St. Joseph. It's no surprise that every other license plate hails from Indiana or Illinois. A mere 90 minutes from the bustle of downtown Chicago, urbanites in search of a summer idyll come here in droves to linger away the sunny days among the ripening grapes.

Tasting rooms, antique shops, espresso wagons, and artisan galleries fill once-vacant storefronts and empty lots in the rural communities north along the Red Arrow, like a wildflower bloom spreading up the shoreline and slowly turning inland along Shawnee Road.

Bicyclists pedal away the miles at the pavement's edge, following decorative wayfinding signs past gently rolling hills carpeted with vineyards and fruit orchards. Each morning, hungry customers crowd in long lines against the glass cases of a local bakery specializing in Swedish pastries. Later in the day, their cars fill the lawns and roadside shoulders in front of quaint country cottages converted into eateries boasting an eclectic array of local fare. Tempting scents drift on the cool lake breeze, mingled with the smoke from campfires at Warren Dunes State Park.

Further inland at the Round Barn Winery just outside the small village of Baroda, families fill hundreds of white chairs and tables scattered across the grass, sipping world-class wines, spirits, and micro-brews and munching gourmet treats while jamming to free music from the open-air stage.

Just a few miles away to the west, the sun sets over Bridgman's Weko Beach where a group of laughing teens light the flame in a paper lantern, then chase it along the sand as it bobs on the wind and begins to rise.

Welcome to Lake Michigan Shore Wine Country, one of the state's most alluring tourist destinations, where the temperate lake effect climate, rolling hills, and rich sandy soils echo the finest wine grape growing regions of France and Germany. A wine lover might easily imagine themselves transported in time and place, back to the early days of Sonoma or Napa Valley, when the world was just catching on that the wine was good from the enchanting countryside merely an hour's drive from San Francisco.

But it wasn't always this way.

HOW IT BEGAN

In the 1970s and 1980s, the little southwest Michigan village of Baroda prided itself on being the per capita leader in the state's tool and die industry, with eight machine shops employing over 220 workers amid a population of less than 900. This wasn't a place where tourists came. It was simply a place where people worked.

As the auto industry shrank and the economy steadily declined, the rural burg seemed doomed to suffer a slow and quiet death. By the time the nation's economy hit bottom in 2008–2009, southwest Michigan had lost over 55 percent of its manufacturing jobs. Only three factories remained in Baroda, employing a scant 61 people.

But Baroda wasn't about to go quietly into the dark.

"In 2004, we realized we needed to do something or Baroda would become another small Michigan ghost town," said Village President Bob Getz. "So we sat down and tried to reinvent ourselves. And the answer was staring us in the face."

What Getz and other community leaders saw were numerous wineries within five miles of the village center, and a richly diverse array of scenic farms, vineyards, and orchards within minutes of a pristine stretch of Lake Michigan shoreline and coastal dunes.

Right then and there, they planted their flag in agritourism and declared Baroda's future as a wine country destination.

In fact, Baroda sits squarely in the center of Lake Michigan Shore Wine Country, a designated American Viticultural Area that stretches across the southwest corner of Michigan from the Indiana border north to the Kalamazoo River. It is the largest of Michigan's four federally recognized wine grape growing regions and ranks 21st in size in the entire country.[1]

According to the U.S. Department of Agriculture – Rural Development, the state's wine grape acreage has doubled in the last decade. Michigan had 32 commercial wineries and 1,300 acres of farmland under wine grape cultivation in 2002. As of 2011, that number had grown to 101 commercial wineries producing more than 1.3 million gallons of wine annually from over 2,650 acres of wine grapes. Michigan now has 15,000 acres of vineyards including juice grapes overall, making it the fourth largest grape-growing state in the U.S.[2]

And it's an industry growing increasingly important to the state's economy. According to the Michigan Wine Institute, Michigan wineries attract more than two million visitors per year, with the industry contributing $300 million annually to Michigan's economy.[3] Overall, Michigan's wine, grapes and grape juice products and related industries produce nearly $790 million in total economic value to the state, paying more than $42 million in state and local taxes and an additional $42 million in federal taxes. The Michigan wine industry accounts for more than 5,000 jobs across the state, with a combined payroll of more than $190 million.[4]

But until recently, wine lovers mostly identified that bounty with the vineyards of the Grand Traverse Bay area; relatively few were aware of what was growing— quite literally—in Michigan's great southwest, as entrepreneurial vineyard owners began switching focus from traditional juice grapes to the world-class varietals used for wine.

In 2002, nearly 20 years after the state's first wine trail was mapped on the Leelanau Peninsula, St. Julian Winery in Paw Paw joined forces with a handful of fellow local vintners to launch the Southwest Michigan Wine Trail organization and began promoting their tasting rooms. The name was changed to the Lake Michigan Shore Wine Trail when the Lake Michigan Shore was designated an official grape growing region in April 2008.

The easternmost point of the Lake Michigan Shore Wine Trail currently starts at Lawton Ridge Winery in Kalamazoo, one of Michigan's newest wineries, then goes as far north as Tabor Hill Wine Port in Saugatuck and as far south as Warner Vineyards' tasting room in New Buffalo near the Indiana border.

Currently, nine are within a five-mile radius of Baroda.

Obviously, Baroda didn't need to plant the vineyards; they just needed to do the economic gardening that would entice investors and entrepreneurs who could create the kind of place that would bring in the people to frequent their businesses.

INVESTING IN A NEW IDENTITY

To help focus their placemaking objectives, they took a long, hard second look at a 2002 market study that had sparked the creation of "casual country charm" as the village brand.

"At the time, most residents said they wanted to keep the small town feel and wanted no commercial development," said Getz. "One of the only things they did want downtown was a supermarket, which wasn't very realistic. Back when I was a kid growing up in Baroda in the 1950s, we had two grocery stores. But that was before the big box chains, when nobody went any place else to shop."

Changing deeply entrenched attitudes is a common challenge in getting community buy-in for placemaking initiatives, said local planning consultant Chuck Eckenstahler.

"It wasn't easy and it isn't easy, and it's always going to be difficult when we are changing a lot of the

basic fundamental precepts of people who have lived here a long, long time," said Eckenstahler who has worked with Berrien County for more than 40 years. "When you talk about placemaking, you always have to ask: how do we reshape the thinking of the resident who says everything's ok and I don't want change? Somehow you have to convince them it's about the economics of what's needed in the future. But there will always be those you can't win over."

By 2004, however, even many of the most nostalgic residents were starting to see that things had to change if Baroda was to survive.

"We saw one little town to the south of us literally vanish. They lost their bank, their post office, their school. They were just gone," said Getz. "At that point, people realized they've got to change their attitude, that maybe you want to see things like they were 50 years ago, but that's just not going to be."

The first thing they did was trade in their much-loved "casual country charm" image for a new logo that was tightly focused on their newfound sense of place: "Heart of Wine Country."

"We've still got casual country charm, of course, but now it's in the heart of wine country," joked Getz.

But how does a tiny village struggling to survive find the resources—and political willpower—for the massive changes necessary to make that image a reality? According to Eckenstahler, the key is "transformational leadership."

"The economics of small and medium-size cities are simply not there for the kind of money necessary to do certain things. As a result there is a reluctance to take on additional risk or very aggressive plans," said Eckenstahler. "When you don't have established projections of growth, private developers

aren't going to take the risk. So to be successful, we have to rethink what our incentives are and how we employ them. The ability of local government to take on a little bit more risk is a necessary incentive to be able to grow the community in the future. But it takes transformational leadership, an action figure in the community, to marshal that message."

Eckenstahler credits Getz with being that figure.

"He was the transformational leader who said 'we're going after the center of wine country and that's the road we're going to march down because that's the only way we're going to have enough tax base to finance what this community needs to survive.' It wouldn't have been possible without that vision."

Village officials then got to work developing a strategic plan to enlarge their Downtown Development District and to use tax increment financing, or TIF funds, to subsidize improvements that would foster private investment and redevelopment in the tiny downtown. They spent the next several years saving and putting aside $350,000 in accumulated TIF funds, which they then parlayed up into $1.4 million in matching grants from the state for road and streetscape improvements, public art, and a low-interest business loan program.

The lion's share was in Michigan Department of Transportation grants for three road improvement projects. A major streetscape project included new paving, sidewalks, street lighting, decorative banners, and flowers along the two main blocks of First Street, the village's dead-end downtown road. Other grants with local funds created gateways into the community from I-94 on the west side and U.S. Route 31 on the east.

Under Eckenstahler's guidance, two tax abatement districts were created, one at the Lemon Creek Road entryway into the village and the other downtown. To encourage investment in capital improvements, each district offers up to 100-percent abatement of local taxes on the increased assessed value of a qualifying business due to building renovations, for a negotiated period up to 10 years.

But they knew they needed something more. In 2008, local officials from Baroda and the neighboring city of Bridgman worked with the Michigan Municipal League in successfully lobbying for an expansion to the state laws on tax abatement districts. Now, when commercial buildings are demolished, the vacant site also qualifies for tax exemptions on site improvements, so that a developer could build a new facility but only pay taxes on the value of the empty lot for an agreed-upon number of years. Baroda is hoping the new tax incentive will entice an entrepreneur to build a bed and breakfast and mixed-use project on the vacant downtown block once occupied by an elementary school.

The next step was developing a tool to help

both new and existing businesses fund the costs of the actual improvements. The Baroda Revolving Loan Fund (RLF) was set up through the USDA's Rural Business Enterprise Grant program. The village provided $50,000 in RLF loans in the first cycle.

The first loan saved the village's last remaining restaurant from going into foreclosure.

"In its heyday in the 1970s and 1980s, Bill's Tap was a very elegant steakhouse frequented by the governor of Illinois and all the Chicago TV personalities. Because of the very strong personality of the owner and extremely good food, it was the place to go for a dinner to see and be seen with the rich and famous of Chicago," said Eckenstahler. "When Bill died, his wife took it over but she just couldn't maintain it alone. About 2008, a gentleman purchased it right before it went into foreclosure. We set up the loan to replace the roof and windows so he could redo the kitchen and interior and reopen as Baroda Tap & Grille. Otherwise, it would've gone into foreclosure and would

be just another derelict building."

The improvements immediately raised the taxable value of the building from $44,100 to $87,400, with an estimated market value in 2012 of $86,600.

Another $15,000 loan funded façade improvements to an old warehouse at Baroda Founders Wine Cellar, creating the village's first wine tasting room.

The taxable value on the partial reuse of the former warehouse building increased from $5,000 to $11,200, with a new estimated market value of $12,400.

"Both buildings were old and needed extensive renovation so we knew we needed to do something to help out if they were going to succeed," said Getz. "These were low-interest, very flexible five-year loans. We gave them each six months to get up and running before they had to make the first payments, and both were paid back in full a couple years ahead of time."

The early repayment enabled the village to make the same offer again, with plans to run ads in the local newspaper for new RLF applicants: "We have $20,000 reasons for you to expand or locate your business in downtown Baroda!"

The village also helped Chicago transplants Bill and Greta Hurst make massive renovations to a former breakfast diner to open Tabula Rasa Gallery, a new boutique art gallery featuring local artists and food products. A tax abatement allowed them to make the improvements without paying taxes on the upgraded value for five full years.

Back in 2005, the couple was living the corporate lifestyle in Chicago, with a vacation home in Union Pier.

"We're avid bike riders and one of our favorite things was to ride out to Round Barn or Tabor Hill winery, drink a bottle of wine and ride back. Obviously, it was a

> "There's no denying that this is an uphill battle. What we're doing here in Baroda is almost an intervention and then a reinvention."

bit of a challenge to ride back," joked Greta Hurst. "We loved it here. It was the land, the wineries, and the restaurant scene in St. Joseph. So in 2005, we bought 11 acres that had been part of an 85-acre orchard, planted a vineyard, and raised chardonnay."

Greta quit her corporate job and in 2007 they began buying income property in the village. They currently own three buildings with five apartments and three commercial spaces. One currently houses a deli while the second has a hair salon on the ground floor and apartments upstairs. The third building houses Tabula Rasa, where they display their artwork and Greta offers yoga classes.

"There's no denying that this is an uphill battle. What we're doing here in Baroda is almost an intervention and then a reinvention," said Hurst. "The rents in the village are very healthy and that's attractive to landlords, but there is no denying there was a fair amount of sweat equity and dollars spent, and maintenance is ongoing."

One challenge cited by Hurst is the overlapping way government units are organized in Michigan, with both a township and a village government levying taxes on the same property owners.

"When you buy income properties to renovate, you have to find that sweet spot, that equilibrium balance where there is positive cash flow. Not everyone is the Warren Buffet of the world who can have a negative cash flow," said Hurst. "There are still a lot of empty buildings and they're very well priced, and there's such a positive vibe in Baroda. So when people come in and see them they want to buy them. The reality is you can get your foot in the door pretty easily, but then you have renovation, double taxation, and the challenge of enough foot traffic year-round to support the business.

It's like pushing a string up a hill with your nose."

Still, Hurst is passionate about her adopted hometown and optimistic about her visions for its future. She's also deeply involved with the Downtown Development Authority, village council, and other civic organizations.

"The people coming for the wineries are our bread and butter. In finding the right businesses to fill the empty storefronts, we have to ask what other businesses these wine visitors want," said Hurst. "I don't think we've reached critical mass yet on food service, and some sort of retail mix: art, food, chocolate, cheese, antiques, kitchen gadgets. We have new blood and younger folks with modern ideas, and we have to embrace technology. There's a lot of opportunity here."

Meanwhile, village officials continue to press forward with their placemaking vision.

An Arts Build Communities (ABC) grant through the Michigan Economic Development Corporation's (MEDC) Rural Arts Program funded the costs for a group of volunteer artists to paint murals depicting wine country scenes on the freshly whitewashed sides of the old feed mill, to beautify the northern entrance into town and heighten its new identity.

The village also invested $45,000 to purchase property adjacent to the mill for future development as a parking lot.

"The goal is to create a large parking area that would create in excess of 100 parking spaces. We believe the mill building will ultimately be repurposed into small shops that cater to the wine tourists and this would create a dual frontage for them," said Eckenstahler. "It would also give us the ability to be more hospitable to large buses and vans and create a more walkable downtown. On most weekends right now

we have two tour buses downtown at any one time. You can't get a fifth wheeler or bus through there right now on a crowded day."

Eckenstahler is now working with the local state representative on legislation that would allow villages the same opportunity as cities to provide additional special liquor licenses in DDA districts based on redevelopment investment rather than population. Right now, only a city with a DDA can do this.

"We have in our plan the potential for up to three additional liquor licenses to be issued to visitor-based businesses as the next step of the redevelopment program, so we can say to a prospective developer a liquor license is available rather than them having to go out and find and buy an available license somewhere, which is extremely difficult."

As of early 2014, House Bill 4257, which would allow a village to issue redevelopment liquor licenses, had passed the House and was sitting in the Senate Regulatory Reform committee.

Other new changes in the way Michigan can make, sell or purchase beer, wine, and liquor are in various stages of the legislative process. In early 2014, the state approved House Bill 5046 allowing bars and restaurants that already have liquor licenses, to let consumers bring their own bottles of wine and to charge corkage fees (BYOB). The measure is supposed to help Michigan's wine industry by allowing consumers to bring local bottles to an eatery which may not carry them.

"But HB 4257 is still necessary to address the larger issue of the availability and expense of the liquor license itself," said Eckenstahler. "The problem is it costs too much front-end money for a person to start a small business, especially one where you rely on 60 days of true full-scale tourism and half-tourism trade for about

30 days on either side," he said. "If Michigan wants to be a tourism destination, liquor licenses need to be less costly and easier to get rather than letting the customer bring in their pre-purchased liquor. Liquor sales may make the business profitable and should be a business income stream."

Another missing piece is that Michigan's new BYOB law only applies to restaurants that already have liquor licenses. Some BYOB laws in other states also allow consumers to bring their own alcoholic beverages to establishments without liquor licenses.

"That expansion would make it easier for an entrepreneur unable to acquire or afford a liquor license to still run a profitable restaurant that enhances dining options in a wine country region, and encourages the sale of local wines," said Eckenstahler.

Other recently passed laws include HB 5140 and HB 4277. HB 5140 allows specially designated distributor (SSD) liquor licenses (typically held by grocery, drug, and convenience stores that sell alcohol) to be transferred within counties rather than only within the municipality where it was originally issued.

Once its tie-barred companion bills are also passed, HB 4277 will allow certain businesses to obtain temporary liquor licenses while awaiting final approval on a license application.

Several other bills being considered would relax restrictions on breweries and brewpubs and enact more flexible liquor licensing.[5]

Meanwhile, Baroda's potential for new wine country-related development was made dramatically plain to see with the 2012 opening of the Round Barn Brewery & Public House on the formerly desolate southernmost block of First Street. The facility is the latest venture by the Moersch family, Baroda natives who also operate the hugely successful Round Barn Winery, Free Run Cellars, DiVine Distillery, and several related tasting rooms in southwest Michigan. By taking advantage of a 10-year tax abatement, they were able to invest $750,000 to renovate an abandoned tool and die shop into an upscale pub with a gleaming, high-tech 36-ft steel bar inside and another outdoor "beer garden," each featuring 20 different draft beers on tap, and wines and spirits from the family's other businesses. The village even relaxed local zoning and building codes to allow them to build the outdoor seating area right up to the property line.

Owner Christian Moersch said that the family's initial investment is already paying off, with doubled beer production in less than one year.

A steady growth trend is occurring throughout Baroda's small downtown. The occupancy rate for the first two blocks of Main Street (zoned for retail) was 44 percent in 2004. In 2013, it was at 70 percent and include four anchors (Round Barn Brewery's Public House, Baroda City Mills, Baroda Tap and Grille, and Baroda Founders Winery), two delis, a sporting goods store, hair salon, barber shop, art gallery, insurance agency, heating and cooling business, church, bar, auto repair shop, music store, and leased office space. Occupancy on the third block of Main Street (originally zoned light industrial and now zoned light industrial/commercial) was 40 percent in 2009 and consisted of tool and die shops and related industries. In 2013, occupancy was at 75 percent and included a brew pub and an antique store located in another former factory

DOMAINE BERRIEN

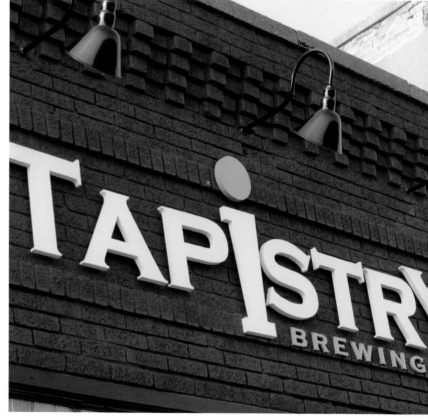

space.

The village is continuing to move forward by applying for a grant from the MEDC for downtown infrastructure funds.

"We are looking forward to the challenges of defining the next phase of growth and development and how to get public infrastructure set plus community consensus," said Eckenstahler. "Progress is not a linear function, but a step function. We now are defining the next big step up—seeking to create another set of big changes. Any time you seek this pathway, you have the challenge of developing strategy, getting community support, arranging the funding, and finally execution of the plan.

"We have the next step strategy pretty much in place, business community consensus in place, and a process defined to gather community consensus sufficient to allow the village council to wrestle with the difficult questions of how to finance another $2.5 million in needed infrastructure to make it all happen. Our application with MEDC would do about half of the strategy in 2015."

THE REGIONAL RIPPLE EFFECT

The placemaking transformation is also encouraging new enterprise in related businesses in the region. In 2006, for example, longtime area resident Steve Salisbury converted his late parents' farm into a quaint vacation rental that now attracts visitors from all over the world.

"I opened the business because I had the property available, and because I saw a need to support the local wine industry with a suitable overnight lodging facility," said Salisbury, an executive business consultant specializing in organization development. Salisbury said he spent about $40,000 to remodel, furnish, and

market Worthenbury Country House, and sales have been consistent at about $20,000 per year for all eight seasons.

Events are also starting to draw visitors from a rapidly growing radius. In 2012, Midwest Elite Racing spent $2,600 with an additional $2,000 from participating wineries and breweries to host 112 runners for the Wine Trail Half-Marathon, with a reported economic impact of $36,000 in visitor accommodations and meals.

The 2013 Wine Trail Half-Marathon had 507 registered runners from 16 states, two Canadian provinces, and Australia. The combined expense was $22,950, returning a direct economic impact of $100,000 in visitor accommodations and meals.

The new focus on tourism doesn't seem to be hurting the village's remaining industrial base. Select Tool & Die owner Mike Conrad said his company's sales have increased an average of 30 percent annually for the past five years, with 2013's total sales higher than the years prior to the 2008 recession when he expanded the business with a 3,000 square foot addition, new parking lot, and the purchase of an 11,000 square foot storage building.

Rose's Concrete saw new construction in 2013 at the highest level since 2008, with 80 percent of the business growth in private homes. Plans are in the works for a second warehouse and storage building.

"When I took over as village president in 2002, our streets were pretty much deserted and we continued to go downhill for years until Baroda was just a shadow of itself by 2008," said Getz. "Now I get calls all the time from people looking for buildings."

During one typical month in late summer of 2013, Getz was fielding calls from a man interested in a hardware building with room for three new storefronts and warehousing in back; a woman wanting to open a

VILLAGE OF BERRIEN SPRINGS
RED ARROW HIGHWAY
WINE COUNTRY
COLLABORATIVE EFFORTS
PLACEMAKING TRANSFORMATION

store selling wine glasses; and a new wine entrepreneur who had recently bought 40 acres to plant vineyards and wanted to put in another wine tasting room.

"If we get enough tourists, I have someone who's requested a gourmet coffee shop, and all the wineries are pushing for overnight accommodations of some kind," said Getz. "And we still have a couple of old tool and die shops where I'd love to get some more manufacturing in. We have plenty of buildings to do both in Baroda."

PARTNERS IN PLACE

The same kind of placemaking transformation has also been happening directly to the west in nearby Bridgman along the Lake Michigan shore. Just as Baroda reinvents itself as the agricultural "heart" of wine country, Bridgman is revving up its identity as its beachfront gateway.

The city of Bridgman began in the mid-1850s as the site of a lumber mill. When the mill was destroyed by fire and the lumber industry moved on, mill founder George Bridgman decided to stay. Instead of cutting trees, he and other residents began growing fruit trees, grapes, and berries. In 1869, the Chicago Michigan and Lakeshore Railroad came through Bridgman's coastal property, erecting a depot in exchange for a reliable water supply for the trains. The depot and post office were officially named Bridgman in 1871.

Manufacturing became the chief economic engine for the region, but local nursery and produce businesses flourished, too. Just south of town along the Red Arrow Highway in neighboring Harbor Country, nearly 2,000 acres of massive beachfront sand dunes were preserved as Warren Dunes State Park, making it a true vacation destination. Tourists began arriving in droves from Chicago, eager to enjoy the pristine sand and water

and the lively resort town atmosphere amidst scenic rolling hills carpeted with grape vines and orchards.

From the Roaring Twenties through the early 1940s, Bridgman's Weko Beach was hopping. People came from all over Chicago and South Bend, Indiana for the legendary Friday night fish fry and dancing at the Weko Beach pavilion.

But things began to change in the years following World War II. In 1945, the pavilion owners dissolved their partnership and the beach house changed from social venue to concession stand. The city purchased the deteriorating property from the township in 1958. A renovation completed in 1991 retained little of the original structure: the foundation itself and the wood floor of the large room overlooking the lake.

The economy was changing too. Since 1980, Berrien County has lost over 50 percent of its manufacturing jobs—jobs that were the lifeblood of Bridgman and its neighboring communities of Baroda and Berrien Springs.

The nearby communities and townships began working on collaborative efforts to promote a new shared "wine country" identity.

A regional wayfinding signage campaign was the combined effort of the city of Bridgman, Lake Township Economic Growth Alliance, village of Baroda, Oronoko Township, Baroda Township, and the village of Berrien Springs. Together, they adopted a master plan to install approximately 46 decorative signs along the Lake Street/Shawnee Road corridor linking the communities from the Lake Michigan shoreline inland to the east, to identify local businesses, amenities, and tourist attractions. The project was led by Bridgman-Lake Township Economic Growth Alliance, a partnership launched in 2005 by the city and township in cooperation with the Bridgman Area Chamber of Commerce. The organizations have since been consolidated into the Greater Bridgman Area Chamber of Commerce and Growth Alliance for better use of human and financial resources, with Baroda acting as an adjunct player in the consolidated organization to continue the regional wayfinding efforts.

"Most towns that are successful in this region have Lake Michigan, but not all of us have that. So we combined our resources and came up with a package program to advertise the whole area," said Getz. "It used to be one little town against another. Now we've got a regional thing. Everybody has their own logo. Bridgman is the beach and Baroda is agriculture. Berrien Springs is culture because that's where the first county courthouse is and lots of other historic buildings."

The first welcome sign was erected in September 2012 at Exit 16 off I-94 along northbound Red Arrow Highway. The second of the wayfinding signs followed shortly, facing into southbound traffic. Eventually, each town will have a kiosk too, with directions to all the wineries, beaches, and other amenities and attractions.

As the national love affair with wine and local foods continues to bloom and grow, agritourism is becoming a major socioeconomic driver for the entire southwestern corner of the state. And the little towns of Bridgman and Baroda are cashing in.

From 2004 to 2012, Baroda's DDA taxable valuation dropped from $6.8 to $5.3 million, mainly due to the large-scale loss of its manufacturing companies. It could still be another year or more before the new socio-economic wave turns those numbers around. But placemaking's impact is already clearly evident in other measures.

Between the 2000 and 2010 U.S. Census, Baroda's population grew at the rate of 1.75 percent while the state's average fell at a rate of 0.55 percent. Baroda's median household income grew by 3.97 percent, more than double the state average of 1.67 percent.

During the same time period, Bridgman's median household income grew by 5.42 percent, more than triple the state average growth rate of 1.67 percent.

In Berrien County itself, which encompasses both communities and their shared core section of Lake Michigan Shore Wine Country, household income grew 10.52 percent in that same decade, while the median house value has increased 43.19 percent compared to 6.66 percent statewide.[6]

"You have to think outside the box, and communicate your plans very well. Let your people know what you're trying to do. You'll end up getting a whole lot more support if you do," said Getz. "Sure, they may express some negative opinions, but they'll appreciate being included. Bottom line is they have to buy in too or it's not going to be successful."

"You also have to be willing to take the long view. Remember, we started with a community questionnaire in 2002, so it's been an 11-year process so far," said Getz. "You just have to promote and take advantage of the little successes along the way. We try to get as much press as we can out of every little project, with a grand opening for each thing. It doesn't have to be huge. And it doesn't happen overnight."

(ENDNOTES)

1 American Viticultural Areas, Wine Institute, accessed, August 27, 2013, http://www.wineinstitute.org/resources/avas.

2 Department of Agriculture & Rural Development, "USDA Report Confirms Significant Growth in Michigan's Wine Grape Industry," accessed, August 28, 2013, http://www.michigan.gov/mda rd/0,4610,7-125-1572_28248-289666--,00.html.

3 Michigan Grape and Wine Industry Council, Michigan's Grape & Wine Industry Fast Facts, Updated April, 2013, accessed August 27, 2013, http://www.michiganwines.com/fast-facts#sthash.MOsyvRqA.dpbs.

4 Michigan Grape and Wine Industry Council, About the Michigan Wine Industry, accessed, August 27, 2013, http://www.michiganwines.com/about#sthash.ExlHDXx4.W2DrzzV6.dpbs.

5 Melissa Anders, Mlive.com, "Gov. Rick Snyder signs BYOB wine legislation, more flexible liquor license rules" mlive.com, December 27, 2013, accessed April 1, 2014, http://www.mlive.com/business/index.ssf/2013/12/michigan_wine_liquor_licenses.html.

6 USA.com Business Intelligence, Baroda, Bridgman and Berrien County, MI, accessed August 29, 2013, http://www.usa.com/.

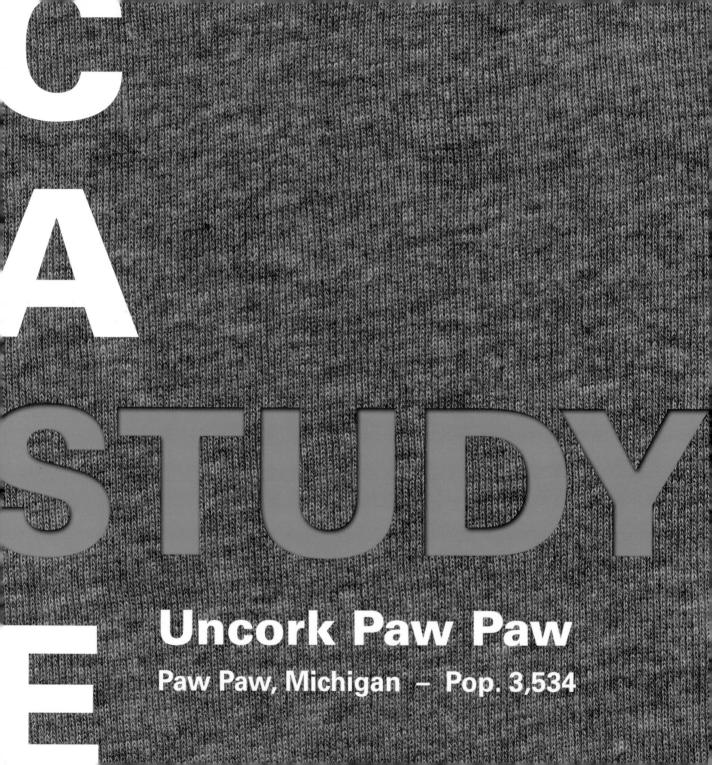

CASE STUDY

Uncork Paw Paw

Paw Paw, Michigan – Pop. 3,534

PROJECT SCOPE

Paw Paw, situated midway between Detroit and Chicago, is home to a growing wine economy. The small village of 2.5 square miles is tucked into the heart of St. Julian Winery (Michigan's oldest and most awarded winery), and Warner Vineyards. Both attract more than 40,000 visitors per year. In addition, Paw Paw entices visitors to its historic downtown with offers of great restaurants, unique shops, and a microbrewery.

As part of a comprehensive strategic plan to grow its local economy, Paw Paw has been utilizing community assets in a way that leverages small businesses through a mix of grants, research, marketing, and business development. New events in the downtown and on the lake are all part of a branding strategy that contributes to the town's unique sense of place and defines it as a Midwest wine country destination.

The St. Julian Winery joined forces with a handful of fellow local vintners to launch the Southwest Michigan Wine Trail organization, which is now called the Lake Michigan Shore Wine Trail. Recognizing their proximity to thousands of households and prospective consumer demand, this community and region saw the potential to grow their business opportunities, and came together to build on their identity as a wine country destination. The village launched a market and cluster analysis to identify a target audience, which was then used to devise an effective strategy for promoting the region and its many seasonal events through billboard ads, radio advertising, local and regional print advertising, direct mail, and appeals. At the same time, they created a proactive support system for new entrepreneurial ventures and existing businesses, giving out more than $800,000 in grants for everything from education and training to building façade and interior improvements.

Village Manager Larry Nielsen said, "I hope that the program will serve as a 'doable' example for other communities seeking to build a sense of place based on their own unique assets, and find the same great success that Paw Paw and its region have experienced."

INVESTMENT

>> Conducted a market and cluster analysis, researching comparable communities to identify gaps.

>> Several local loans and grant money were made available for local businesses through Façade Grants, Business Development/Challenge (BDC) Grants, and Training and Educational (TG) Grants.

• Façade grants can go to any business in their Downtown Development Authority (DDA) district with a maximum of $10,000 in any one year, or $25,000 in five years.

• The maximum BDC grant is $5,000, and the TG grant is $1,000 in a year. The BDC and TG grants are only available to business owners with less than 10 full-time employees. Loans can be made for up to $25,000.

>> 337 grants and 11 loans have been awarded since March 2009.

>> 107 different properties/businesses have been recipients of these grants, for a total of $878,000.

>> Future plans include embarking on enhancements to their downtown to make it more walkable and pedestrian-friendly.

SOCIOECONOMIC IMPACT

>> The region began to flourish.

• Between 2009 and 2011, there were 47 ribbon-cuttings for renovations, expansions, and new businesses; between 2011 and 2013, 44 additional ribbon-cuttings took place.

• Between 2009 and 2013, 18 commercial and service businesses and new mom-and-pop stores were started.

• 105 full-time equivalent employees were added, with some as part-time seasonal employees.

>> The tax base in the Paw Paw DDA before the recession was $17.5 million, and through the tough years they never fell more than 3 percent. Today, the tax base has increased by 5.5 percent. Businesses felt that this aggressive marketing and grant program made a difference in their survival and growth, even during the challenging times.

LESSONS LEARNED

>> When embarking on a project, don't make assumptions about anything. Let the data do the talking. You will be surprised by what it shows.

>> Don't underestimate the entrepreneurs you have in your very own community. It's important to identify those individuals.

>> When recruiting businesses to your community, test and refine your pitch and be prepared to give them data. They want numbers to back up your proposals.

For additional information, visit:
www.uncorkpawpaw.com

Chamber of Commerce
Tel: 269.657.5395
Email: info@pawpawchamber.com

Downtown Development Authority
Tel: 269.415.0060
Email: m.springer@pawpaw.net

Moving Placemaking Forward Through Agritourism

• Viticultural Area – a delimited grape-growing region for an American wine destination having distinguishing features as described in the Code of Federal Regulations (CFR) at 27 CFR Part 9 and a name and delineated boundary as established in Part 9 of the regulations. The establishment of viticultural areas allows vintners to describe more accurately the origin of their wines to consumers and helps consumers to identify wines they may purchase.[1] To find out how to petition for a designation, check out the Manual for Petitioners.[2]

• Tax Increment Financing (TIF) – a popular funding tool that can finance the public costs associated with development and redevelopment projects. TIF occurs when a local government freezes the tax base within a specific development district and uses the revenues generated by reassessment or new development to finance selected improvements within the district. The term "tax increment" refers to the additional taxes that will result from private development. This "increment" is earmarked or "captured" for the TIF for purposes of economic development instead of going to other taxing units that otherwise would receive the revenues. Public improvements can be financed one of two ways in a TIF plan: 1) Improvements may be financed on a pay-as-you-go basis from annual tax increment revenues 2) The municipality may issue tax increment bonds to finance public improvements and use the annual tax increment revenues to retire the bonds.[3] The Michigan Municipal League provides a list of current TIF tools in a One Pager Plus.[4]

• Michigan Department of Transportation (MDOT) grants – MDOT offers a wide range of grants for road improvements. [5]

• Commercial Redevelopment Act – this act expanded the state laws on tax abatement districts in 2008. It allows for tax exemptions for new, replacement, and restored facilities in city and village redevelopment districts. Under 1978 PA 255 (as amended by 2008 PA 227), a legislative body is authorized to exempt a commercial property (replacement facility, restored facility, or new facility) from certain parts of the General Property Tax Act. A facility issued a certificate is exempt from real property taxes and is instead subject to a new commercial facilities tax.[6]

• United States Department of Agriculture (USDA) grants – USDA's Department of Rural Development provides grant funding to the state of Michigan to encourage the growth of businesses in rural communities.

The grants are awarded to private businesses, government entities, and nonprofit organizations to support business planning, start-up, infrastructure, and the use of sustainable technologies.[7]

• Michigan Economic Development Corporation's (MEDC) Rural Arts Program – This program recognizes that an arts-based economy can improve the quality of life, generate revenue, attract visitors, and encourage investment. MEDC provides a grant-funding opportunity that targets communities with a population of 15,000 or less to highlight rural art projects. Grant funds to qualifying communities range from $5,000–$10,000 with a 50/50 local cash match.[8]

• Liquor Licenses – Although current Downtown Development Authorities (DDAs) can already get a redevelopment liquor license so long as they meet the redevelopment dollar threshold and there are no available quota licenses, there is pending legislation in the Michigan Legislature to fix the current redevelopment liquor license to allow DDAs in villages and townships to have these licenses, a practice already being done by the Michigan Liquor Control Commission, but not expressly allowed in law.

• Lake Michigan Shore Wine Trail – This collaboration of more than a dozen wineries and tasting rooms in southwestern Michigan is marking its 10th anniversary. Together this group forms a wine trail that promotes locally produced wines, tastings, and events. The region, known among wine connoisseurs as the Napa Valley of the Midwest, is an American Viticultural Area (AVA) similar to other acclaimed wine producing areas in California and upstate New York. More than 10,000 acres of grapes grow in the Lake Michigan Shore AVA which stretches across the corner of southwestern Michigan from the Indiana-Michigan state line, up the coast of Lake Michigan to the Kalamazoo River, and east to the city of Kalamazoo.[9]

• Façade Improvement Program – This program is handled through the MEDC using Community Development Block Grants (CDBG). It is structured to provide funds for commercial/mixed-use building façade improvements to minimize deterioration of traditional downtowns. This program is based on the premise that the exterior improvements will stimulate additional private investment in the buildings and the surrounding area, and attract additional customers, thereby resulting in additional downtown economic opportunities.[10]

(ENDNOTES)

1 Alchohol and Tobacco Tax and Trade Bureau, American Viticultural Area (AVA), February 11, 2013, http://ttb.gov/wine/ava.shtml.

2 "Registration Manual for Petitioners," United States Tax Court, November 2008, http://www.ustaxcourt.gov/eaccess/eAccess_Registration_Manual_for_Petitioners.pdf.

3 Michigan Association of Planning; http://www.planningmi.org/downloads/tax_increment_financing.pdf, 1986.

4 "Economic Development Tools – Financing Tools, One Pager Plus," Michigan Municipal League, January 2011, http://www.mml.org/resources/publications/one_pagers/opp_economic_development_tools-financing.pdf.

5 Michigan Department of Transportation, http://michigan.gov/mdot/.

6 "Commercial Redevelopment Act, One Pager Plus," Michigan Municipal League, http://www.mml.org/resources/publications/one_pagers/opp_commercial_redevelopment_act.pdf.

7 Serena Cassidy, "Grants to Start a Rural Business in Michigan," eHow, http://www.ehow.com/info_781142_grants-start-rural-business-michigan.html.

8 Pure Michigan, Michigan Council for Arts and Cultural Affairs, 2013.

9 Lake Michigan Shore Wine Country; http://www.lakemichiganshorewinetrail.com/news/299-lake-michigan-shore-wine-country-kicks-off-10th-anniversary-by-adding-two-new-wineries-to-its-wine-trail.html, 2013.

10 "Michigan Community Development Block Grant Community Development Initiatives," Michigan Economic Development Corporation, 2013, http://www.michiganbusiness.org/cm/files/fact-sheets/cdbg.pdf.

The ability of art to create a sense of place is older than the Sphinx and the pyramids of Giza. It's the essence of awe in the Sistine Chapel. It's the cultural force that drew the best and brightest to the Left Bank of Paris in the 1920s, and to New York's Greenwich Village in the fifties.

In today's world, it can be experienced in the throbbing techno beat of Detroit's urban core; in the vibrant desert colors of Santa Fe; in the sounds and crowds of South by Southwest in Austin; and in the flavors and smells of Seattle's Pike Place Market.

It can make a place absolutely unique, unmistakable, and irreplaceable. That's the placemaking power of arts and culture. There is nothing that speaks more directly to the core of what it means to be human, nothing else that pulls us with such fascination and allure.

If you're looking for a shortcut to create a sense of place, this is it. Just be sure that what you're doing is genuine and authentic. Anything less will taste as flat as fast food and be as worthless as a cubic zirconia.

But once you've got it: pure gold.

Creative State Michigan shows that in 2011, nonprofit arts and cultural organizations contributed over half a billion dollars in expenditures to Michigan's economy. Arts and culture bring significant value to the state's economy, and also attract and retain professional talent and business investment. Creative State Michigan reveals that for every $1 invested by the state, the arts and culture nonprofit sector contributed $51 into the Michigan economy. The benefits are not just short term. From 2006 to 2010, the number of arts-related jobs increased by 15 percent in Michigan, while arts-related businesses increased by 65 percent.[1]

Got art? No? Well, better get it.

(ENDNOTES)

1 ArtServe, "New Data Reveal Significant Impact by Michigan's Creative Sector," accessed March 12, 2014, http://www.artservemichigan.org/20120125113/news/artserve-announcements/new-data-reveal-significant-economic-impact-by-michigans-creative-sector/.

CHAPTER PHOTO CREDITS:
MICHIGAN MUNICIPAL LEAGUE
TRAVERSE CITY FILM FESTIVAL

ARTS + CULTURE

RETURN OF THE LAST PICTURE SHOW

How Traverse City is Making Movie Magic

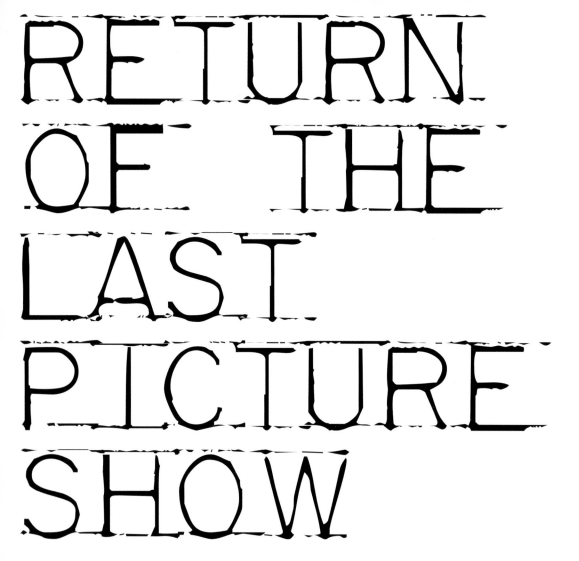

Back in the 1990s, people came to Traverse City mostly for the cherries and the waterfront along the bay. Wine touring on the Leelanau and Old Mission peninsulas was just starting to catch on in this northern Michigan resort community. A brand new shopping mall, chain restaurants, and high-rise hotels sprawled at the city's edges.

Seasonal tourism was hopping in and around the "Cherry Capital of Michigan" and a growing number of wealthy residents vied for space to build their northern getaways along the scenic shoreline outside town. But the true, historic downtown business district had been displaced and drained of vibrant life, mostly ignored by the traffic speeding past on its way to somewhere else.

"The big watershed event was the construction of the mall in 1991, which lured away JC Penney and left a large space downtown," said Traverse City Downtown Development Authority (DDA) Executive Director Rob Bacigalupi. "When I arrived about 15 years ago, downtown was not in bad shape; our vacancy rate was maybe only 8 or 9 percent. But the retail base was very tourist-oriented and very seasonal, without much of the diversity that appeals to your actual residents."

Like most American cities in the decades following WWII, Traverse City's downtown business district had seen the range of its "retail repertoire" gradually narrow as the malls and "big box" stores of suburban sprawl replaced the traditional downtown retailers that people frequented for their personal and household needs.

As early as 1979, local civic and business leaders saw what was happening and looked for ways to recharge the city's faltering heart. The DDA, Traverse City Parking, and a volunteer business organization known as Downtown Traverse City Association (DTCA) were merged under one umbrella organization known as Downtown Traverse City. Each arm was charged with specific tasks in an organized effort to recruit new retail and office development, improve infrastructure, and develop events and marketing campaigns to bring people back downtown.

Sometime around 2004, Traverse City Light & Power tore down an old coal power plant along the West Bay waterfront, creating what is now known as the Open Space, which many credit with spurring new development on the west side of town. But by 2005, however, the central business district was still struggling to fully shed its lingering souvenirs-and-tee-shirts image that offered little interest to year-round residents.

STATE OF THE STATE

The most potent and poignant symbol of what had been lost was the once-grand State Theatre on East Front Street. Originally built in 1916 as the Lyric Theatre in the golden age of silent films, the grandiose movie house was also an active community center in its heyday, providing a popular local venue for weddings and other community events. The brightly lit marquee of the 1949 incarnation of the theater, now renamed the State Theatre, had served as a familiar beacon above this much-loved gathering place for generations of local residents.

It was the place to be at midnight on March 20, 1929 when a new era in cinema dawned in northern Michigan. For the first time in the region's history, audiences watched as the Lyric's curtain rose on Lucky Boy starring George Jessel, a "talking" picture that would help mark the end of silent films. The special showing also included a brief clip of Herbert Hoover's inauguration speech, an equally important landmark event.[1] For the very first time, local residents were able to see and hear their president speak to them from the nation's capital hundreds of miles away.

After its second major fire in 1949, the movie palace was rebuilt and renamed the State Theatre. But gradually, people forgot what was so special about the picture shows that once drew them together in the magic of the dark. Like so many old movie houses across America, the State Theatre closed down for good in 1996 after a modern multiplex cinema opened at Grand Traverse Mall. For years, the State sat shuttered and forlorn, while local nonprofit groups struggled to come up with a way to salvage the classic structure as a performing arts complex.[2]

Then Hollywood came to town.

But Oscar-winning filmmaker Michael Moore didn't set out to bring glamour and glitz to the city when he built his home near the northern resort community. Instead, he brought a placemaking vision that began with one simple idea born from his own background and experience—movies are made to be a communal experience, and a really good place to see really good movies can become a community's vital core.

First, Moore and two fellow local film fans—author Doug Stanton and photographer John Robert Williams—launched a weeklong film festival. The inaugural event debuted in 2005 with 31 films at 52 screenings over a 5-day period, with 50,000 admissions.

While Moore's celebrity no doubt helped get the project off the ground, the group accomplished the feat by simply using the assets already available in the community, like any other grassroots effort—a local community playhouse, the restored city opera house, a school auditorium, and of course, the then-vacant State Theatre.

In a 2013 interview with Interlochen Radio, Williams described the partially restored facility at that time as a "hodgepodge mess of old wood here and there" with cheap, plastic fold-down seats and no carpet.

RAVERSECITY FILMFESTIVAL

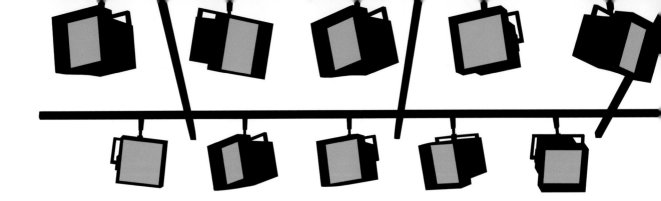

Volunteer crews worked tirelessly to clean it up in time for the festival's 2005 premiere. The theater's mini-metamorphosis was like a bit of movie magic in its own right, a beacon of things to come.

"One night, we suddenly got the marquee lights running out front," Williams recalled in the interview. "People were stopping, taking pictures, cars were going by honking their horns, yelling, giving thumbs-up. It was like this dead old ship had suddenly come to life. Even though it was not that pretty on the marquee, it was there. And I think that spark and that flame that started drawing people downtown is the one critical point that can't be missed in all of this now. If you saw the State Theatre with the marquee dark, you'd wonder what was wrong."[3]

As Humphrey Bogart said in Casablanca, it was "the beginning of a beautiful friendship."

Two years later, in 2007, Rotary Charities mortgaged the building for $1 to the nonprofit Traverse City Film Festival (TCFF), the community-based nonprofit set up to own and operate both the theater and annual festival as community assets. Moore and a small handful of local philanthropists kicked in the bulk of the restoration money out of their own pockets, bolstered by countless smaller donations from the community at large. Over the next six weeks, hundreds of craftsmen and local volunteers hung curtains and hammered nails in a massive, total restoration of the theater, complete with a new balcony, 540 new made-in-Michigan seats, state-of-the-art sound and projection, and the biggest screen within 150 miles.[4]

"Some people think we're lucky and it just 'happened.' But we believe very strongly that when Michael Moore came to town and looked at the State Theatre, one of the big factors in the decision was that we had built a parking deck that was right around the corner," said Bacigalupi. "He knew that in order for 500 people to want to come see a film downtown instead of at the mall, it had to be relatively convenient for people to get there."

In other words, an infrastructure "garden" had been created where a project like the State Theatre could thrive.

On Saturday, November 17, 2007, the State Theatre officially reopened with the northern Michigan premiere of The Kite Runner.

It is a movie experience almost unknown in

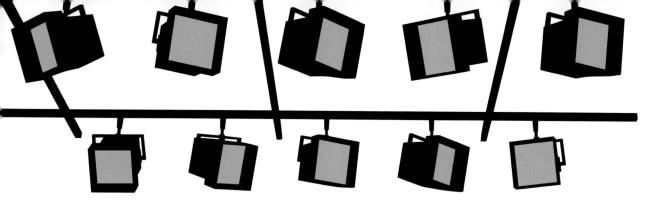

today's environment of generic pillbox cinemas. At the start of every film, a massive red velvet curtain rolls up to unveil the 50-foot screen, and a theater organ rises up out of the stage. Thanks to the work of Northwestern Michigan College astronomy instructor Jerry Dobek, the ceiling is dotted with thousands of tiny fiberoptic lights replicating the stars and constellations that actually fill the night sky above the Traverse City State Theatre in August.

"Michael has dedicated a huge portion of his life to the film festival, the State Theatre, and the Bijou by the Bay," said Deb Lake, executive director of the Traverse City Film Festival. "He truly loves movies, and believes in the importance of seeing movies on big screens, with great sound, in beautiful theaters together with other movie lovers. He pays careful attention to each and every detail of the movie-going experience—he picked out the seats, the carpet, the candy and popcorn we sell at the concession stand, even the kind of straws we use."

Since its grand reopening in 2007, the State

Theatre has consistently been one of the top-grossing independent art houses in North America, managing to stay in the black even as movie attendance continues to drop nationwide. In its first six years of operation, the State Theatre was constantly among the top 10 movie theaters in North America for weekly ticket sales. It was in the top 10 theaters for highest weekly grosses 181 times for the movie it was showing in a given week, and it was the number one highest grossing theater in North America a stunning 83 times.

MORE THAN MOVIES

The nonprofit, year-round movie house also serves as a model of community engagement and grassroots socioeconomic development, with the entire operation run by a small crew of full-time professional staff who are paid a living wage with full benefits. There is also a revolving cast of community volunteers working as concession counter and box office clerks, ushers, and clean-up crew, in exchange for soda and popcorn, the chance to see a movie for free, and the simple satisfaction of being part of the city's movie magic.

That level of community ownership makes it possible for the operation to adhere to Moore's foundational belief that everyone should be able to afford to go to the movies. Adults can see a first-run movie for

$6 to $8; students are less. Late-night Friday Night Flicks movies are two for $5. Saturday morning kids' matinees are 25 cents–crowd-pleasers that often bring in full houses and feature monthly bike giveaways sponsored by the Grand Traverse Pie Company. Everyone can enjoy 25-cent classic movie matinees on Wednesdays. Popcorn and soda are $2 each. Candy is as low as $1. Each week, the theater offers an average of 2.5 free screenings. And each year, if the temperature rises above 100 degrees fahrenheit, everyone gets in free.

"This is the community's theater. Like in a co-op, everyone pitches in as a volunteer," Moore wrote in a June 5, 2013 entry on his blog, michaelmoore.com. "Volunteers pop the corn, take the tickets, and run the box office. Community groups pick the shift they'd like to work each month, which means on any given night you'll have a county judge and a single mom working the concession counter, the high school English staff working as the ushers, and the Boy Scout troop on clean-up. Everybody gets free movies tickets for this— and the knowledge that they are the true 'owners' of this theater."[5]

"The theater is a magnet, drawing residents together and turning strangers into friends," said longtime resident and retired Traverse Bay GISD Career Tech Center teacher Donna Valdmanis. She has frequently volunteered at the State Theatre, both individually and as part of a group, and has been a film festival volunteer for nearly every year of its existence.

"I've met so many people there that I can't imagine where else I would've met them. I'm always meeting new people," Valdmanis said. "I just love the idea that it's volunteer-led."

Valdmanis said the State has also expanded her world in unexpected ways.

"I've even gone to the opera there, and that's something I've never done before in my entire life," she said. "It was some kind of live feed from the Metropolitan Opera in New York. It's just amazing that I can do that on a Saturday afternoon right here in northern Michigan."

Five and a half years after reopening its doors, the State's box office sold its one millionth admission ticket in June 2013, a mind-boggling feat in a city of only 16,000 year-round residents. Two weeks later, the film festival staff held a ceremonial mortgage burning to celebrate assuming full ownership of the facility after five solid years of successfully honoring all the stipulations that had been set forth in the 2007 mortgage with Rotary Charities.

In May 2013, the Motion Picture Association of America named the State Theatre the #1 World's Best Movie Theater, ranking it above iconic world-class venues in France, Australia, Greece, India, Thailand, Spain, and South Korea.[6]

The ripple effect has been profound in the few short years since the theater's reopening.

"What it did was extend the shopping into the evening hours," said Bacigalupi. "We've always struggled to get merchants to stay open late. What the theater did was bring a lot of people downtown in the evening and many stuck around for dinner or drinks, and that put more people on the streets in the evening, and so the shops started staying open later too."

"The increased downtown foot traffic has acted as a catalyst to spark more programming at other downtown venues such as the Opera House and Old Town Playhouse, more live music and dining options, and more events, which in turn has attracted more diverse and upscale retail," Bacigalupi said.

"Many people refer to the State Theatre as a magnet drawing people to downtown Traverse City," said Lake. "Business and restaurant owners tell us all of the time about people who come in daily, saying they've just been to see a movie. On average, the theater welcomes 400 people daily, people who might not otherwise come downtown."

Meanwhile, the city has invested heavily in infrastructure and streetscape improvements throughout the downtown area. From 2008-2010, nearly $8 million in private donations renovated the city-owned Opera House. In 2009, the DDA used Community Development Block Grant funds (CDBG) to bolster a $7.9 million investment to build the Old Town Parking Deck. This played an integral role in retaining the downtown headquarters of Hagerty Insurance, which employs more than 400 local people. In 2013, the opening of the new Bijou by the Bay was enhanced with a $3 million investment in improvements to Clinch Park by the DDA, Traverse City Light & Power, the Department of Natural Resources (DNR) Trust Fund, and private investors. The improvements included expanded public access, bathrooms, a concession stand, and a water park attraction directly across the street from the central downtown district.

"One of the most significant impacts the city had on building a vibrant city center is our zoning code, particularly not requiring parking," said Planning Director Russ Soyring. "Per our zoning code, we even make it more difficult to build private parking lots. Developers need to prove there is not public parking available within 500 feet of the site. This all allows for a more compact, rich, mixed-use environment that makes the place interesting and fun."

"Two private developments, Midtown and

The resulting transformation is nothing short of remarkable. Today, all along Front Street and for blocks in every direction, downtown Traverse City is thriving.

River's Edge, have utilized public financing, including Community Development Building Grants and Brownfield funding, to spur tremendous revitalization that has completely changed the look and feel of the area in and around Cass, Lake, and Eighth Streets," said City Manager Jered Ottenwess.

The resulting transformation is nothing short of remarkable. Today, all along Front Street and for blocks in every direction, downtown Traverse City is thriving. Eclectic art shops and boutiques, locally owned eateries, coffee shops and bars, new and renovated office buildings now cozy up against each other in and around a colorful urban hub that combines the best of classic small town Americana with a trendy, vibrant feel that rivals any resort town on the continent.

"Fifteen years ago there were maybe 15 or 20 coffee shops and restaurants downtown. Now we have 55. We also have a lot of strength in women's apparel, accessories, and jewelry," Bacigalupi said. "Our retail vacancy rate is virtually zero now, to the point where it's a problem because there's no place for businesses to expand. Hopefully, the market will take care of that as developers build more to accommodate the tremendous demand for retail space."

And downtown Traverse City isn't just for tourists anymore. Area residents who once shunned the old Front Street business district are back in force.

"I don't remember going downtown much at all before. We were just going to the malls. The State gave me a reason to go downtown," said Valdmanis, who has lived on Old Mission Peninsula for more than 30 years. "I feel like in the last two or three years, so many restaurants, shops, breweries, and boutiques have moved to downtown. Now there's so much to do and we usually do several things at one time. We'll go to a movie and then we'll stop in a few stores, go for lunch or dinner. It isn't just a one-stop for us. We make a deal of it."

But even those most integral to the city's hip new indie film image are quick to point out all the elements that came together to make such a success story possible.

"For many years, leaders in our community have nurtured downtown and planned great things for Traverse City. The vitality downtown enjoys today is not solely due to the film festival or the State," said Lake. "But most people recognize that the State and the festival have had dramatic positive effects on the city and its economy. New businesses, events, nonprofits, and services have sprung up. People have been inspired to do great things in part because of what we've done. It's very important to us that the State and festival do everything we can to make our community stronger and better, that we continue to help make Traverse City a place where young people want to stay and entrepreneurs want to start businesses."

BIJOU BY THE BAY

In order to help make the State sustainable and to allow it to better serve the community, the film festival opened a much-needed second screen, the Bijou by the Bay, in time for the 2013 film festival. July 29, 2013 saw the completion of the $800,000 first phase of a major renovation of the city's 80-year-old Con Foster Museum in Clinch Park on the beach across the highway from one of the main downtown parking lots, just a block away from the State.

Lake said that the Bijou is run by the same staff and volunteers that run the State. It will continue the film festival's mission of improving the area's quality of life, enhancing access to the arts, and stimulating a more vibrant local economy with expanded downtown programming. By giving the State Theatre the "second screen" it has needed for so long, it helps meet the growing demand for more great movies, for an affordable night out, and something for our young people to do.

Unlike the State Theatre, which is deed-restricted to showing only films that open on fewer than 200 screens across the U.S., the new venue will be able to show any first-run movie, including blockbusters. Having a second screen will also allow the nonprofit group to bring more new films to the State, by allowing them to move films over to the Bijou to fulfill distributor obligations. The smaller 150-seat venue will also be better suited than the massive 540-seat State to screening foreign films, documentaries, classics, and obscure films.

Besides expanding the city's fast-growing movie culture, the renovation also saved an important historic landmark. It was originally built by President Roosevelt's Civil Works Administration in 1934, and named for an iconic figure in Traverse City's history.

Aptly enough, Conrad H. Foster, 1875-1940, was Traverse City's first great theater manager. The Boston native arrived in northern Michigan in July 1917 to manage the Lyric Theatre. Described as a "true showman with a passion for the movies,"[7] Foster began by installing a newer and brighter screen in the Lyric as part of his publicly stated commitment to making the theater one of the best in the state.

After his employers transferred him to another movie house in Wisconsin, Foster spent six years petitioning the company to return him to his post in Traverse City. That happened in April 1924, when

he placed this ad in the Traverse City Record Eagle newspaper[8]:

> "My ambition has been to return to Traverse City, since they made me leave, to operate what I think is the most beautiful theater in our circuit. I have come to love the city, its good natured folks, and have often told my wife that Traverse City is the place to make a home. So it is with great pleasure that I can announce that my longings have been realized and I have again been transferred to the best little city in the world."

For the next 16 years, Foster dedicated himself to making the Lyric the best movie house in the state. He was instrumental in bringing the first "talkie" to northern Michigan in 1929, and installed state-of-the-art sound and projection equipment that was virtually unheard of in cities of comparable size.

Foster's impact on Traverse City didn't begin and end at the door to his movie house. He was an enthusiastic cheerleader for the Cherry Festival and served the city in many capacities, including city commissioner and as a member of the Chamber of Commerce.

It was in 1934, during his stint as the city's first parks commissioner, that Foster came up with the idea of cleaning up the waterfront on the shoreline site of a closed lumber mill, and replacing it with a public park with a zoo, beach house, and historical museum. For the next several years, he traveled more than 15,000 miles across the Midwest buying Native American and pioneer artifacts for the proposed museum's display.

When Foster died of a heart attack in 1940, downtown businesses closed for his funeral, and then Gone with the Wind was screened at the Lyric. On the day of his death, the Record-Eagle published this tribute: "When Con Foster died this morning, a part of Traverse City died with him, not a physical part, but a spiritual part."[9] In appreciation for his efforts on behalf of his adopted hometown, Con Foster's name was carved into the museum building, without his prior knowledge, shortly after the building was completed in 1934.

Eventually, the Con Foster Museum collection grew to over 10,000 artifacts and was moved to a larger home. Today it is part of the History Center of Traverse City, housed at the Grand Traverse Heritage Center. But the original city-owned brick structure on the shoreline remained empty, too significant to tear down, but without a clear idea for its future usefulness.

Buoyed by the State Theatre's overwhelming success, in 2013 the City Commission unanimously granted the nonprofit TCFF permission to renovate the long-vacant museum in similar fashion. Again, rather than rely on tax dollars, they turned directly to the community for the necessary funds. A large portion of the $350,000 was donated by local benefactors Richard and Diana Milock, who were also among the small core group of primary sponsors of the State project. Other project funds were donated by a group of Bijou Founders who each gave $50,000; seat sponsors who donated $1,000 per seat; brick sponsors who donated $500 per brick; and donations in other amounts from hundreds of individuals.

With a publicly-stated mission to open in time for the 2013 festival and, at the city's request, to finish construction during the larger Clinch Park renovation the city had undertaken for the spring and summer, work began in earnest in early June 2013. Construction crews replaced rotted roof trusses and removed asbestos from the ceiling. Next, they stripped the interior to the outer walls and dug out the floor to create a slope for theater seating. Displaying the same community spirit seen in everything else connected to the film festival, subcontractors voluntarily donated many items and services to keep the project within budget, and a group of volunteers pitched in to complete the huge renovation.[10]

Today, the name Bijou by the Bay glows in art deco marquee lights above the somber tan brick doorway that covers, but does not obliterate, Foster's name. A historic marker outside the theater lets everyone know who Con Foster was and the importance he had in Traverse City's history. And there's little doubt the late showman would have been delighted to see the building that once housed his museum become the home of this new movie house on the water, owned and celebrated by the entire community.

"Everybody was on board with doing what they could to make the Bijou happen. Now you can see some life back into it and the whole Clinch Park area as well," said Valdmanis. "It's beautiful down there now. Now I feel like it's a place I could go and have lunch and walk around. It's a new part of being downtown."

A PLACE FOR FILMMAKERS AND FANS

If the State Theatre has become the physical heart of Traverse City's cultural revival, the Traverse City Film Festival is the lifeblood that keeps it pumping with a beat that's grown louder and more exciting with each passing year—loud enough, in fact, to be heard around the world.

On August 6, 2013, Taiwanese filmmaker Arvin Chen (Will You Still Love Me Tomorrow? and "Au Revoir Taipei") praised the festival on his Tumblr blog, Filming People is Easy, with this entry that was then shared by an international audience of fellow bloggers[11]:

I just got back from the Traverse City Film Festival in Northern Michigan. It's amazing. Having attended a pretty wide range of festivals, including some of those "prestigious" international festivals, this is the one that really made me appreciate movies (including my own) again. How did this happen?

It's a weird festival in a lot of ways—it takes place in a small tourist town on Lake Michigan, one of those summer towns I've only read about or seen in movies, but never visited. On the surface, it seems more appropriate for a big Fourth of July celebration or something, not an international film festival. Traverse City is pure Americana…there's a Main Street USA (Front Street) with a beautiful 100-year-old single-screen theater, several bookstores (as in more than one, seriously!), there are stores selling fudge, ice cream, kettle corn, and the famous local cherry-jams and the city is, by my estimate, about 99.9 percent white (I might have been the entire .1 percent).

The founder is Michael Moore, and at some point over nine years ago, he decided to bring indie films, foreign films, and some pretty hard-core documentaries to this small town in Middle America. But instead of just using Traverse City as the backdrop for the festival, he decided to make it part of the town…really getting the community involved and making it "their" festival as well. As a result, the festival is run (very effectively) by almost entirely local volunteers. Only two or three of the staff is full-time and paid. And they're way better at their jobs than most festival staff. Also, they don't accept film submissions. Michael and a few of his programmers hand-pick movies from other festivals, or get recommendations.

I don't think I've ever felt as appreciated as a filmmaker or maybe even as a human being. Michael made a short but moving speech at the filmmaker lunch about cinema being the most popular art form and how important it is to him that filmmakers are treated with that respect (as artists) at this festival. They really backed it up:

Every single screening is packed (even theaters with 800-seat capacities), and the sound and projection are by far the best that I've had so far on this festival/theatrical run. There's a theater manager at every screening that literally sits with you once the movie starts until you've told him if the sound and projection quality is okay with you. Somehow, they managed to have other (much better) filmmakers come and moderate the panels and Q&A's, so they're really leading discussions about filmmaking. They put the name of the movie up on the marquee for every screening. They have a filmmaker lounge constantly stocked with food and refreshments donated by local restaurants. You can get tickets to any screening just by asking (I've never seen so many other movies at a festival ever). The people in Traverse City are so nice they will stop you on the street and compliment you about your movie and thank you earnestly for coming to the festival, so nice that when you're crossing the street, they'll roll down their car windows and yell "I loved your movie." I played with

*the festival volunteers in a fucking
kickball game!*

*I've definitely already doused
myself in the Kool Aid. I left Traverse
City hoping that I would make
another movie soon only so I might
have another chance to go back to
Traverse City.*

It would be easy to shrug off the entire
phenomenon of the festival's success by saying that it's
the beloved brainchild of a wealthy and famous Academy
Award-winning filmmaker and author—implying that such
stories are only possible in a community lucky enough
to have a local benefactor of Moore's caliber. But by all
accounts, including Chen's, a crucial part of the event's
success is the enthusiastic participation and support of
the city government, a community of generous business
and individual sponsors, and the residents themselves.
Rather than the achievement of a single person, it is
solid proof of the power of civic engagement.

A veritable army of more than 1,500 volunteers
runs the show, putting in over 20,000 combined hours
on tasks from cleaning up litter to crowd control and
answering phones. A team of 250 volunteer managers
donate more than 40 hours per week to overseeing the
festival's operations. During the entire weeklong event,
"Information Ambassadors" are seemingly everywhere,
inside the venues and outside on the streets, ready with
a friendly smile and well-rehearsed answers to visitors'
random questions. If you stand still and look lost for
more than a few minutes anywhere downtown, it's
practically a given that someone in a commemorative
volunteer tee shirt is going to ask if there's something

they can do to help.

"Sure it's incredibly helpful to have an
internationally known Oscar-winning filmmaker running
the show, but what we do would not be possible without
our stellar group of dedicated, talented, wonderfully
trustworthy volunteers," said Lake, who also started as a
volunteer in the festival's inaugural year.

It's a success that has grown with each passing
year.

Opening night features a street party of epic
proportion, with a full block of live music and local
wineries and restaurants offering up their culinary
specialties beneath the State's glowing marquee. In
2013, hundreds of partygoers lined up more than an hour
early at $50 per head for the chance to mix and mingle
with filmmakers and fellow fans.

Anyone doubting the festival's impact as an
economic driver need only see the crowds milling along
the sidewalks, cruising in and out of the open doors of
every shop and eatery downtown.

In 2013, the ninth annual Traverse City Film
Festival broke more records than ever before, logging
119,000 admissions over 6 days. The festival offered
102 feature films and 52 short films. Ninety filmmakers
from four continents were on hand for screenings, 10
film school sessions, 10 panel discussions, seven free
industry panels, and five public parties. A total of 123 of
188 screenings of the American and foreign films were
entirely sold out. Nearly 1,500 volunteers worked more
than 20,000 hours to provide a fun, safe, and friendly
experience for visitors from around the world. More
than 80 musicians from all parts of the globe played
at different venues throughout the week at a variety
of gala events. Shopkeepers hosted sidewalk sales
and competed for prizes with movie-themed window

1,500 VOLUNTEERS

20,000 COMBINED HOURS

119,000 ADMISSIONS OVER 6 DAYS

250 VOLUNTEER MANAGERS

INFORMATION AMBASSADORS

displays.

While other film festivals seek to model themselves after Cannes and Sundance, catering to the exclusive and elite, the Traverse City Film Festival prides itself on being inclusive. Even as its fame and popularity grows with each passing year, the organizers remain committed to keeping it a common people's event that will not alienate the residents of its own home community.

The "festival on a budget" options include free movies in the Open Space park at dusk; free filmmaker panels at the City Opera House; free movie fan discussions at the Cinema Salon; a free music stage on the beach in Clinch Park; $1 kids' films following a free lawn party; $5 film school classes; free movies for volunteers; and public after-glow celebrations for those who can't afford tickets to the official festival parties.

As part of its mission as a charitable educational organization, each year the festival also donates DVDs of the films shown to local public libraries, which then loan them for free to library patrons.

The result is nothing short of a citywide love affair. In 2013, the festival added 60 new sponsors, with a 40-percent increase in sponsor dollar support. Even before the 2013 festival had ended, new "Friends of the Traverse City Film Festival" memberships were already pouring in for the 10th anniversary in 2014.

"Most who come to Traverse City for the film festival come specifically for that event. It has created a different kind of awareness of Traverse City from a cultural standpoint, that we're not just a beach town or wine country destination. It's bringing people involved in the film industry and others who likely wouldn't have come here otherwise. And once they come and enjoy it, they tell others," said Brad Van Dommelen, president and CEO of Traverse City Tourism.

Lake agreed.

"People who are interested in art and culture, entertainment and movies, and the world come to see the movies we bring. And when they get here to Traverse City, they fall in love with our amazing community," said Lake. "Every year we hear about people who moved here after visiting the festival. Then they start businesses and patronize businesses, and it all keeps getting better."

"The success of the film festival, the excitement generated downtown, and the feeling people got when the State Theatre reopened and lit up Front Street with that magical glow all changed the perception people had about the city. It was somehow cooler and more exciting. And it's all had a dramatic effect on downtown, with hundreds of people shopping and eating downtown on a daily basis who otherwise wouldn't have been doing that."

Those successes have encouraged an ever-expanding calendar of annual events that together have helped extend the city's tourism season into virtually a year-round affair.

"Events and festivals in themselves are only a small part of the whole thing as to why people come here, maybe less than 5 percent of the reason, but our events play a huge role in building a positive vibe for Traverse City," Van Dommelen said. "They may come for the wineries, Sleeping Bear Dunes, or the beaches as the primary reason. But once they get here and find out these events are happening, it ratchets up significantly to like 25 percent who say they participate in those events once they're here."

The reverberating impact flows in both directions.

"Traverse City is very different from the tourist destination it was 10 or 20 or 30 years ago. We're no longer tiny little mom-and-pop motels along the bay. We've matured and evolved to have different types of lodging facilities, and a wine and foodie culture that's creating a whole different atmosphere," said Van Dommelen. "Ten or 20 years ago, had anyone tried to start a film festival here, it probably wouldn't have worked because the type of economy that would attract those types of people didn't exist here yet."

Regardless which chicken or egg came first, the sum of all these factors is a booming tourism industry that generates billions in spending at local businesses and employs thousands of local residents.

According to a 2013 report commissioned by Traverse City Tourism, there were 3.3 million visitor trips to the Traverse City area in 2012, with $1.18 billion in total spending at local businesses.[12]

"There's no question our tourism industry has grown. One of the major things is the growth in out-of-state business in the last five years. In 2005, 87.5 percent of our visitor volume was in-state. It was 71 percent in 2013," said Van Dommelen.

The socioeconomic impact is far-reaching, well beyond the initial tourism dollars spent.

"The reason employers are able to recruit high-caliber professionals to a small city in northern Michigan, is because of the downtown we have, the restaurants, the wineries, the events, all those sorts of destination attributes that make it a great place to live. We've become a destination of choice for highly skilled people who could go anywhere, but they choose Traverse City," Van Dommelen said. "It's something we try to help people understand. Our economy here is so tourism-centric, and it runs so broad and deep, it's hard to look at anything happening here without looking at how that has been driven by tourism."

Meanwhile, the future just keeps getting brighter for the nonprofit that just a few short years ago seemed like nothing more than one eccentric filmmaker's whimsical pet dream.

In the 2011 fiscal year (the most recent year posted on Guidestar.org), the Traverse City Film Festival organization posted annual revenues of over $2.8 million, and provided $2.6 million in program services that included operating costs for the Traverse City Film Festival ($1.3 million), State Theatre ($1 million), and Comedy Arts Festival ($131,662), as well as a grant to Traverse City Area Public Schools for auditorium renovation and library programs ($139,665).[13]

Obviously, not every community has a celebrity activist to provide the cultural catalyst, or a ready handful of wealthy benefactors to underwrite costs and simplify the necessary fundraising. But the overwhelming success of the State Theatre, Bijou on the Bay, and the festival itself has shown what is possible with vision and passion, even if it is on a smaller scale. The ripple effect has helped spark similar projects elsewhere in the state, such as the Vogue Theatre in the city of Manistee, and the Redford Theatre in Detroit.

In fact, seeding those efforts has become part of the nonprofit organization's core mission.

"It is true that our community is special and the person who started our festival is special. And it's true that by the time we did the State, the film festival had already built up film literacy in the area and had an army of volunteers. All those things contributed to our success," said Lake. "But it also created a model that you can put in a bottle and take to other communities and replicate it. That's why we have a proactive program to share our business model.

"People from all over the country call us about their abandoned theaters to ask how we did it. How do you get the volunteers? How did you raise the money for renovations? What popcorn popper do you use? We're always happy to answer those questions and share our original business plan," Lake said. "Often they'll send people here and we'll take them on tours to meet the staff, the volunteer coordinator, give them the lowdown, and share documents like our volunteer handbook and employee handbook to save them some time."

In July, 2014, Moore announced plans to go even further in supporting independent and small-run films, and the community theaters that want to show them. His $250,000 donation will seed a nationwide program to simulcast some of the films shown at the State to 300 small theaters across the U.S. and Canada. As for Traverse City itself, the accolades just keep on coming: "America's Top Five Foodie Towns" by Bon Appetit Magazine in 2010.[14] National Geographic's "Best Summer Trips of 2012."[15] USA Today's "Ten Great Places to Get the Scoop on Ice Cream" in 2011.[16] "America's Top 10 Wine Destinations" by TripAdvisor.com in 2009.[17] AOL Travel's list of "America's Best Beach Towns" in 2010.[18] Midwest Living's "Best Midwest Food Towns."[19] Livability's "#1 Foodie City"[20] and "#4 Best Winter Vacation Destination."[21]

"We're all about our community and making it stronger. We want companies nationwide to come here and provide great jobs. If we can help raise the quality of life for those employees and make it more likely for them to stay here than go someplace else, we're doing our job," Lake said.

TRAVERSE CITY FILM FESTIVAL BY THE NUMBERS [22]

THE 2013 FESTIVAL
>> 119,000 admissions
>> 102 features, 52 shorts
>> 188 screenings at 10 venues
>> 90 filmmakers from four continents
>> MI Filmmaker Award – Paul Feig
>> Bijou by the Bay opens
>> 13 free screenings added at Compliments of the Festival

THE 2012 FESTIVAL
>> 91,000 admissions
>> 93 features, 117 shorts from every continent but Antarctica
>> 167 industry guests
>> MI Filmmaker Award – Winsor McCay

THE 2011 FESTIVAL
>> 128,000 admissions
>> 156 screenings
>> 147 films (88 features and 59 shorts) from every continent but Antarctica
>> 130 industry guests
>> Dutmers Theater for experimental film added
>> Renovation of Lars Hockstad Auditorium
>> First year of Kids Fest on the lawn outside Lars Hockstad Auditorium
>> MI Filmmaker Award – Sue Marx

THE 2010 FESTIVAL
>> 106,000 admissions
>> 80 films and 40 shorts from over 25 countries at 135 screenings
>> Second annual film school, doubled in size
>> Five free panel discussions and six outdoor movies
>> 70 industry guests
>> MI Filmmaker Award – John Hughes

THE 2009 FESTIVAL
>> 96,000 admissions
>> 71 films and 50 shorts from over 30 countries at 123 screenings
>> New film school, new kids fest
>> Five free panel discussions and outdoor movies
>> 65 film industry guests
>> MI Filmmaker Award – Rich Brauer

THE 2008 FESTIVAL
>> 80,000 admissions
>> 71 films at 108 screenings
>> Three student workshops and students shorts
>> Five free panel discussions and outdoor movies
>> 50 film industry guests
>> A new 400-seat venue
>> MI Filmmaker Award – Kurt Luedtke

THE 2007 FESTIVAL
>> 80,000 admissions
>> Six days long
>> 66 films at 98 screenings
>> Two student workshops and short films by student filmmakers
>> Five free panel discussions
>> 30 film industry guests
>> A new 900-seat venue
>> MI Filmmaker Award – Christine Lahti

THE 2006 FESTIVAL
>> 70,000 admissions
>> 67 films at 95 screenings
>> A student workshop and short films by student filmmakers
>> Six free panel discussions
>> 40 film industry guests
>> MI Filmmaker Award – Jeff Daniels

2005 INAUGURAL FESTIVAL
>> 50,000 admissions
>> Planned in a two-month span
>> 31 films at 52 screenings
>> Four free panel discussions
>> 10 film industry guests

(ENDNOTES)

1 "State Theatre History," The State Theatre, accessed August 12, 2013, http://www.statetheatretc.org/about/history-of-the-state-theatre/.

2 Ibid.

3 Brad Aspey, "50 Years of Big Ideas: The Refurbished, State-of-the-Art State Theatre," Interlochen Radio, July 24, 2013, http://interlochenpublicradio.org/post/50-years-big-ideas-refurbished-state-art-state-theatre-0.

4 Michael Moore, "I Built a Movie Theater–and a Film Festival–and I'd Like You to Come to it," Huffington Post, July 15, 2012, http://www.huffingtonpost,com/michael-moore/traverse-city-movie-theater_b_1674126.html.

5 Michael Moore, "Here's How we Built a Movie Theater for the People–and Why the MPAA Says it's #1 in the World," Huffington Post, June 5, 2013, http://huffingtonpost.com/michael-moore/heres-how-we-built-a-movi_b_3391123.html.

6 Bill Keith, "10 of the World's Best Movie Theaters," Motion Picture Association of America website, May 20, 2013, http://www.thecredits.org/2013/05/ten-of-the-worlds-best-movie-theaters/.

7 Sally Michel, "Con Foster History," The State Theatre History Committee, accessed August 20, 2013, http://www.anotherhundredyears.org/con-foster-history.

8 Ibid.

9 History Center of Traverse City, "The Museum," accessed August 20, 2013, http://www.traversehistory.org/TraverseHistory/The_Museum.html.

10 Brian McGillivary, "Budget for Bijou is $900,000," Traverse City Record Eagle, July 19, 2013.

11 Arvin Chen, "Best Film Festival Ever?", Filming People is Easy (blog), Tumblr, August 6, 2013, http://filmingpeopleiseasy.tumblr.com/post/57474925790/best-film-festival-ever.

12 Scott D. Watkins, Colby Spencer Cesaro, and Samantha Superstine, Anderson Economic Group, LLC, "Tourism-Related Benefits in Traverse City's Economy," Commissioned by Traverse City Tourism, August 28, 2013.

13 Nonprofit Report for Traverse City IRS 2011 Form 990, accessed November 5, 2013, http://www.guidestar.org/organizations/20-3100410/traverse-city-film-festival.aspx.

14 Kate Bassett, MyNorth.com, http://www.mynorth.com/My-North/September-2010/Bon-Appetit-Loves-Traverse-City/ September 23, 2010.

15 Carlos Osorio, AP, National Geographic Online, accessed August 23, 2013, http://travel.nationalgeographic.com/travel/best-trips-summer-2012/#/traverse-michigan-summer-trips_52799_600x450.jpg.

16 Larry Bleiberg, USA Today http://travel.usatoday.com/destinations/10great/story/2011/05/10-great-places-to-get-the-scoop-on-ice-cream/47702444/1, May 10, 2011.

17 Brooke Ferencsik, TripAdvisor.com, http://multivu.prnewswire.com/mnr/tripadvisor/37975/, September 22, 2009.

18 Jordan Simon, AOL Travel, http://news.travel.aol.com/2010/06/18/americas-best-beach-towns/, June 18, 2010.

19 Midwest Living, accessed August 23, 2013, http://www.midwestliving.com/travel/around-the-region/best-midwest-food-towns/?catref=cat6470006&page=4.

20 Livability, accessed August 23, 2013, http://livability.com/top-10/top-10-foodie-cities/traverse-city/mi.

21 Livability, accessed August 23, 2013, http://livability.com/top-10/top-10-best-winter-vacation-destinations-americas-hottest-cold-cities/traverse-city/mi.

22 Traverse City Film Festival website, accessed August 22, 2013, http://www.traversecityfilmfest.org/about/#numbers.

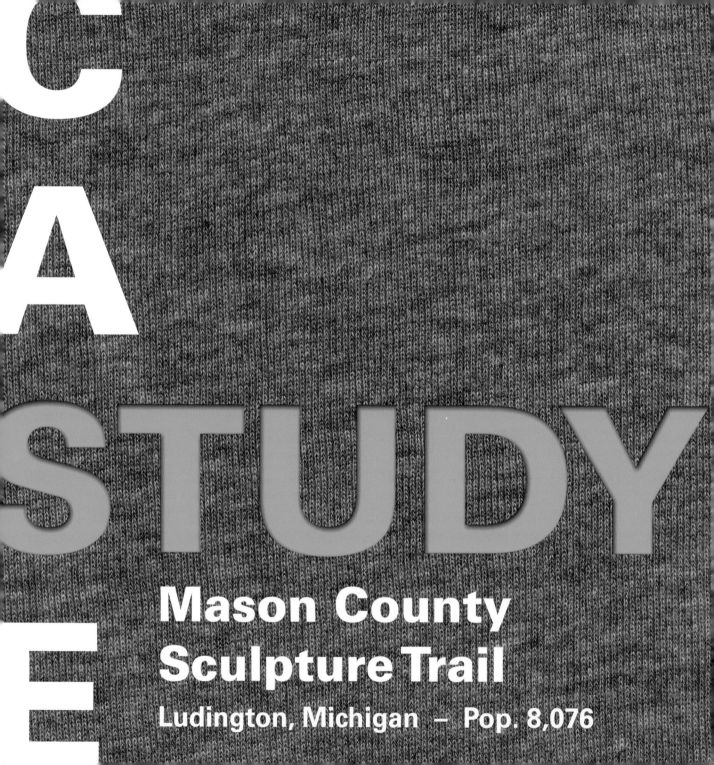

CASE STUDY

Mason County
Sculpture Trail

Ludington, Michigan – Pop. 8,076

PROJECT SCOPE

What started out as one person's dream and vision over 10 years ago, has become a catalyst for change not only for the city of Ludington, but for the region as well. Loveland, Colorado, a mecca for artists with over 200 sculptures, was the inspiration for the creation of Ludington Waterfront and Sculpture Garden, a sculpture park along a splendor of public waterfront space.

With an expanse of green space stretching along the city's harbor, it was ripe for something magnificent to happen. Turning the open space into a cultural attraction has created a real destination by the water. Known for its natural beauty along the Lake Michigan shoreline, this small Michigan city and its region have become a year-round cultural destination that enjoys recognition for its strong agricultural, maritime, and lumber heritage. In addition to the sculpture garden, a playground, band shell for music and events, and a condominium development have added to the vitality and richness of this waterfront. The importance of connecting the park to downtown was acknowledged by creating pedestrian walkways.

Momentum continues to build through the regional Cultural Economic Development Plan that was spearheaded and developed by an 11-member task force.

The plan states, "Among a breadth of ambitious goals aimed at invigorating our creative economy and enriching our quality of life and spurring economic growth, we intend to build off our strengths by creating a sculpture trail throughout the county".[1]

With the success of the city's sculpture park enjoyed by residents and visitors throughout the year, the regional sculpture trail in the works will expand to the city of Scottville, and the villages of Custer, Freesoil, and Fountain. This will be funded through grant money as well as funds raised by the individual communities.

But it doesn't stop there. The sculpture park has been the inspiration for other cultural celebrations, with plans underway to convert the historic Coast Guard Station building into the Port of Ludington Maritime Museum, dedicated to the region's charter fishing industry and Coast guard rescue operations. There are also plans to create a Ludington Maritime Heritage Park and county Agritourism Trail.

This small city on the beautiful shores of Lake Michigan is already putting itself on the map as a premier cultural destination.

INVESTMENT

>> Countless volunteer hours of mobilizing and engaging the business community, residents, local officials, neighboring communities, and artists.

>> Individuals and businesses have purchased the various sculptures ranging from $25,000 to $150,000.

>> Just under $10,000 of city funds is earmarked to maintain the park on a yearly basis.

>> The development of a regional Cultural Economic Development Plan spearheaded by an 11-member task force, focusing on cultural tourism.

>> Preparation of grant proposals to solicit funds for the expansion of the regional sculpture trail.

>> Ongoing communication to the residents through the distribution of a digital newsletter that informs, presents strategies, and provides progress reports on all cultural arts projects in the region.

SOCIOECONOMIC IMPACT

>> With the development of the Cultural Economic Development Plan for the city and Mason County, Ludington is becoming a cultural tourism destination.

>> Cultural arts were used to engage residents and surrounding communities to create a better quality of life and grow the economy.

>> A richer, interactive cultural experience for the visitor was created through the use of audio/video/QR Code.

>> Cultural tourism has become a catalyst for multiple downtown revitalization efforts and events.

>> As part of the regional sculpture trail, the small village of Fountain (pop: 193) has already found the perfect place for its sculpture and a way to engage its residents. Located across from a convenience store, (where you can buy ice cream cones and sandwiches), which serves as the community hub, the village plans to create a plaza with picnic tables where the sculpture will showcase the area's lumbering heritage. It will be a gathering place for people of all ages to enjoy.

>> The regional impact is being felt with residents of neighboring states investing in individual sculptures.

>> As part of the Cultural Economic Development Plan, a total of five trails will celebrate the environment and heritage of the region with synergy and connectivity.

>> Forging a partnership with Michigan State University to develop a platform to measure the impact of the cultural economy.

>> Ludington Waterfront and Sculpture Garden is listed in the International Directory of Sculpture Parks and Gardens. Information on sculpture parks, sculpture gardens, outdoor university collections, sculpture trails, and earthworks from around the globe can be easily located within this site either by location or by name search.[2]

LESSONS LEARNED

>> Identify the leaders and stakeholders in your community to not only support your vision but become potential sources of funding.

>> Reach out to develop public/private partnerships.

>> Educate the community upfront on why investing in cultural arts is a critical component in growing the economy, creating a quality of life, and contributing to the emotional attachment one feels for their community.

>> Be serious about the visitor experience by engaging them physically and mentally.

>> Identify what defines your community (heritage, people, products, etc.) and celebrate it through cultural events.

>> Devise different ways in which to measure the real economic impact where possible. For example, look at the increase in visitors, home values, increase in sales, new businesses, etc. This is important to do from the onset.

>> Be open to new ideas when traveling around the state, country, and world which can lead to inspirations for your own community.

(ENDNOTES)

1 Cultural Economic Development Plan for Mason County, accessed April 22, 2014, http://www.ludington.mi.us/departments/community_development/cultural_economic_development.html.

2 International Directory of Sculpture Parks and Gardens, accessed April 22, 2014, http://www.bbk.ac.uk/sculptureparks/.

Moving Placemaking Forward Through Arts + Culture

- Downtown Traverse City – This organization includes the Downtown Development Authority (DDA), the Downtown Traverse City Association (DTCA), and Auto Parking Services which is unique in terms of structure and operational funding. The DDA was created in 1979 and levies two mills within the DDA district. The DTCA, a voluntary organization of merchants and other businesses, was organized in the 1960s and serves as the marketing arm for downtown. In 1990, the two organizations signed a management agreement merging their offices and staff. Aside from improvements in financing and communications, the merger has had the added benefit of creating clear roles for the two organizations. Listed below are the major areas of responsibility:[1]

– The DDA is involved in retail and office recruitment efforts, public improvements such as streetscapes, partnerships with Traverse City Light & Power to bury utilities, and planning and development issues. The DDA also operates the Sara Hardy Downtown Farmers Market. Funded through a two-mill levy and management contracts, the DDA serves as the conduit for funds through contracts and employs all downtown staff. It is governed by a 12-member board appointed by the city commission.[2]

– The Downtown Traverse City Association (DTCA) focuses its attention on marketing and promotion, overseeing all communication pieces including a monthly newsletter, monthly broadsheets, various promotional brochures, and a downtown website.[3]

– Traverse City Parking is a city enterprise responsible for public parking in downtown and other areas of the city. Funding comes from a separate enterprise fund that is self-sustaining.[4]

• Traverse City Film Festival (TCFF) – The festival is a community-based nonprofit organization located in Traverse City, Michigan. Charitable donations to this organization are deductible. The Traverse City Film Festival benefits arts, culture, and humanities, focusing specifically on film and video programs. The organization's IRS foundation code is 170(b)(1)(a)(vi), which indicates it receives a substantial part of its support from a governmental unit or the general public. The Festival is also classified by the IRS as an educational organization.[5]

• Community Development Block Grant (CDBG) – A federal program that utilizes funds received from the U.S. Department of Housing and Urban Development (HUD). Each year, Michigan receives approximately $30 million in federal CDBG funds, which facilitate various projects throughout the state. Funds are used to provide grants to eligible counties, cities, villages, and townships, usually with populations under 50,000 for economic development, community development, and housing projects.[6]

• Brownfield Redevelopment Funding – Brownfield properties are those in which the redevelopment or reuse of the property may be complicated by the presence or perception of contamination. Revitalizing and redeveloping these properties protects the environment, reuses existing infrastructure, minimizes urban sprawl, and creates economic opportunities. The Michigan Department of Environmental Quality administers a grant, loan, and tax capture program to facilitate the redevelopment of brownfield properties.[7]

• Traverse City Zoning code – The code makes it difficult for developers to build private parking lots, unless they can prove that there is not public parking available within 500 feet of the site. This encourages a more compact, rich, mixed-use environment.[8]

• ArtServe's Creative State Michigan – This report details the impact Michigan's arts and cultural nonprofit organizations have on the state's economy and citizens. Creative State Michigan is the source for information on how the arts, culture, arts education, and creative industries contribute to Michigan and its economy. It has recently published its third edition.[9]

(ENDNOTES)

1 Downtown Traverse City, accessed June 5, 2014, http://www.downtowntc.com/.

2 Ibid.

3 Ibid.

4 Ibid.

5 Traverse City Film Festival, accessed June 5, 2014, http://non-profit-organizations.findthebest.com/l/324058/Traverse-City-Film-Festival.

6 "Michigan Community Development Block Grant Community Development Initiatives," Michigan Economic Development Corporation, 2013, accessed June 5, 2014, http://www.michiganbusiness.org/cm/files/fact-sheets/cdbg.pdf.

7 Michigan Department of Environmental Quality (DEQ), accessed June 5, 2014, http://www.michigan.gov/deq/0,4561,7-135-3311_4109_29262---,00.html.

8 Traverse City Zoning Code, Chapter 1374, Circulation and Parking, accessed June 5, 2014, http://www.traversecitymi.gov/downloads/1374.pdf.

9 Creative State Michigan, accessed June 5, 2014, http://creativestatemi.artservemichigan.org/about/creative-state-michigan/.

On February 8, 1965, President Lyndon B. Johnson delivered his historic "Natural Beauty" message calling for the development of a system of trails across the nation's metropolitan areas and countryside.

In heralding trails as the linear parks of the future, the president said: "We can and should have an abundance of trails for walking, cycling, and horseback riding, in and close to our cities. In the backcountry we need to copy the great Appalachian Trail in all parts of America." Three years later, Congress passed the National Trails System Act and the president signed it into law on October 2, 1968.[1]

That was just the beginning.

While federal efforts largely remained focused on national scenic and historic hiking trails spanning long distances, local government and private interests took the lead in developing trail corridors along abandoned railroad beds and other types of non-motorized multi-use pathways and bike routes in and around urban areas.

The results went far beyond mere recreation. In the years since, these amenities have come to be recognized as key assets for any community wishing to offer a high quality of life to its residents, and a wise investment in the future.

When it comes to economic impact, bicycling is big business. According to the 2006 Active Outdoor Recreation Economy Report, 60 million Americans participated in bicycling—double the population of Canada. They spent $6.23 billion in retail gear sales and nearly $50 billion on bike-related travel. Bicycle-based recreation supported 1,135,268 jobs and generated $17.7 billion in federal and state taxes. Total economic impact of bicycling is over $132.8 billion—more than hunting, fishing, and paddle sports combined.[2]

It should be no surprise then, that growing numbers of communities all across the nation are investing in multi-use trails and designated bike routes as an integral part of their placemaking strategy, based on solid economic data showing that bicycle-friendly communities attract residents, tourists, and businesses alike. According to a 2009 Michigan Sea Grant report:[3]

BIKE TRAILS

- 70 percent of Americans say that having bike lanes or trails in their community is important to them.

- Bicycle trails increase home real estate values and support nearby businesses.

- Cycling enhances recreational and social opportunities, especially for children.

- Rural counties with services for tourism and recreation tend to have stronger employment, higher incomes, lower poverty levels, and improved health and education, when compared with rural areas without tourism and recreation attractions.

- 88 percent of bicyclists also participate in other outdoor activities, such as kayaking, running, or fishing.

(ENDNOTES)

1 Thomas L. Gilbert, "The National Trails System: What It Is And How It Came To Be," National Park Service, updated April 4, 2007, accessed February 13, 2014, http://www.americantrails.org/resources/feds/FEDNatTrSysOverview.html.

2 "2006 Active Outdoor Recreation Economy Report," Southwick Associates for Outdoor Industry Association, accessed February 13, 2014, http://www.outdoorindustry.org/images/researchfiles/RecEconomypublic.pdf?26.

3 "Southern Lake Huron Assessment: Charting the Course for the Bluewater Coast," Michigan Sea Grant, Recreation Profile: Biking, revised 2013, accessed February 13, 2014, http://www.miseagrant.umich.edu/wp-content/blogs.dir/1/files/2012/05/Southern-Lake-Huron-Assessment-Final-Report.pdf.

PLACE MAKING ON WHEELS

Trail Breakers

When it comes to the placemaking potential of bike trails, Michigan has obviously been paying attention. It's first in the nation for the total number of open rail-trails (119) and its' 2,653 miles of multi-use trails represent 12.4 percent of all the rail-trail mileage in the country—currently the most miles of any state.[1]

It all began with the Paint Creek Trail, the state's first rail-trail, which opened in 1983 in Southeast Michigan. The trail linked the cities of Rochester and Rochester Hills, the townships of Oakland and Orion, and the village of Lake Orion in Oakland County.

Among the newest is the Noquemanon Trail Network in the Upper Peninsula, a mountain biking single-track system near Marquette that was enhanced and expanded to interface with the region's rapidly growing multi-use trail network.

They're as different as two bike trails can be, yet each has helped pave the way for "trail towns" to become one of the most popular—and successful—placemaking trends in Michigan.

THE PIONEERS OF PAINT CREEK

Once upon a time, the old Detroit and Bay City Railway line was a major transportation route cutting northward from Michigan's industrial center to the heartlands beyond. The railroad was completed from Detroit to Bay City on July 31, 1873, and became the property of the Michigan Central Railroad Company in 1881.[2] But by the 1980s, hardly anyone was left alive who could remember those railroad glory days of the early 1900s when the fare to Detroit was two cents a mile, for a whopping total of $2.18 for the 109-mile trip from Bay City.

"The height of luxury was to train-ride to Detroit in a parlor car equipped with large, roomy, plush-covered swivel chairs. A porter would take care of your luggage, and on entering Detroit, brushed your hat and coat with a whisk broom," recalled Bay City resident Mrs. Harriet Gustin Campbell in a memoir written in 1982. "To sit back in your parlor car seat and look out the window at the passing scene of fields and forests, or farmhouses and the tiny villages, was a restful treat. The day coaches were more likely to be dirty, sooty, and crowded with 'tired' mothers, fretty children, and lunch boxes."[3]

The railroad morphed through several other name changes before ending up as part of the Penn

Central Company in 1968. Soon after, Penn Central stopped running trains down the line. In 1977, it was officially abandoned when the company went into bankruptcy.

About ten miles of the old rail bed ran from the city of Rochester north through Oakland Township toward the village of Lake Orion on its way to Lapeer County and further north to Bay City. The old Detroit and Bay City Railway line was just another abandoned railroad corridor, the rusted iron tracks pulled up for scrap and the weeds growing thick and high, nearly obscuring the narrow banks of Paint Creek meandering along its edge like a silent travel companion, or a ghostly witness to days long past.

But some local residents didn't see it as an eyesore. They saw it as an opportunity.

One of those was longtime Oakland Township resident Peggy Johnson, who served on the Oakland Township Parks and Recreation Commission from its creation in 1974 until 1994.

"My family was enjoying that corridor back when the railroad was still operating. My kids walked along the railway so they wouldn't have to take the bus to school. The boys would come home with frogs and salamanders in their pockets from the Paint Creek," said Johnson, chuckling fondly at the memory. "Myself, I was always riding my horse up and down it. You could hear the train blow the whistle from two miles away so I'd have plenty of time to get my horse far enough off the tracks. It was just a wonderful part of our lives."

Johnson knew she wasn't the only one with an eye toward the rail corridor's potential. In 1973, a survey of Oakland Township residents had shown strong support for pathways and trails. Over in adjacent Avon Township, residents had already approved a millage to build bike paths. The time was ripe for action. In 1974, the new parks commission held its first meeting to talk about the possibility of acquiring the section of rail line running through the township.

The railroad was keenly interested in making a deal but unable to act due to the bankruptcy proceedings. But on October 25, 1978—the day after the bankruptcy officially ended—Johnson got a call asking if Oakland Township was still interested. If so, Penn Central was ready to send a lawyer from Philadelphia to meet with township officials.

Worried the railroad executives might think the Oakland Township officials were "a bunch of unsophisticated rural rubes," they chose to meet instead at the Bloomfield Hills office of attorney George Googasian, an Oakland Township resident who had served briefly as a parks commissioner and continued to offer his services pro bono. Johnson said that although Googasian's private

practice was focused on catastrophic injury and wrongful death cases, he had extensive experience as a mediator and arbitrator and was a valuable ally in the trail acquisition.

"We arrived at the meeting and instead of one lawyer representing Penn Central there were three," recalled Johnson. "George leaned over and whispered to me that you should always have one more lawyer than the other side. Then he rushed out and suddenly rounded up two more attorneys from his law offices so we'd have four attorneys to their three."[4]

Still, the negotiations were hardly a done deal. Penn Central's Chicago-based appraiser came in with a very high initial appraisal that was far beyond the reach of the township's modest funds.

"One thing that helped us negotiate a more reasonable price was that the state of Michigan had passed a law that you could no longer create land parcels that had no road access. That forced the railroad to sell a full mile from road to road, rather than selling off a couple residential parcels at each end at a higher price," said Johnson.

At the same time, local officials all over the nation were recognizing another potential problem for new rail-trails. When the railroads were originally established, the land was given to them with the stipulation that ownership would revert to the original property owners' heirs if the railroad ever abandoned it.

"That was a potential mess, so the Michigan Legislature passed a new law that anyone who wanted those reverted rights would have to do it within a two-year period or they'd be extinguished by the new state law," said Johnson. "We didn't have any direct threats to the Paint Creek Trail, but there were some cases beginning to arise and we were very aware there was always that possibility."

With negotiations firmly underway toward a lower price, Oakland Township leaders met with those of Avon Township, the city of Rochester, and Orion Township to form the Paint Creek Trailways Commission. More than 200 people showed up for the first public meeting.

Most were excited at the possibilities for a recreational trail through the community. Not so for many of the property owners who were actually adjacent to the rail corridor. Their concerns ran the gamut of fears that homeowners typically express when faced with a public access uncomfortably close to their own private boundaries.

"A lot of fears of the unknown were expressed. Would trail users stay on the trail or trespass into their backyards? Would the trail become a route where robbers could come and break in our back doors? What's been the previous experience with such trails? All those questions were asked at that original public meeting," said Johnson. "Sometimes the honest answer had to be 'we don't know but we'll get the answers and come back to you.' That was the point when we hired Alice Tomboulian."

Alice Tomboulian was a former township board member who had recently completed a term in the State House of Representatives where she'd been deeply involved in environmental issues.

Tomboulian immediately set to work calling trail managers in Wisconsin, the San Francisco Bay area, and other places where bike trails had already been established. In February of 1982, she presented her report, "Responses to Questions Regarding Proposed Yates to Lake Orion Non-Motorized Public Trail." Johnson said that document turned out to be a crucial tool in winning public support:

"She didn't just talk to trail managers. She also talked to police about crime. It was very comprehensive. We gave copies to every member of the city councils and township boards who would be voting up or down on this trail. That way when their constituents starting calling, they'd have the answers right in front of them. That made them very comfortable about making their decisions."

BREAKING GROUND

Once the majority of residents were on board, the Paint Creek Trailways Commission was ready to move forward with buying the property. The newly renegotiated price of $450,000 seemed fair to everyone involved.

At the last minute, the state stepped in offering to help in the acquisition. The problem was that in order to get a matching grant from the state, the state required the purchase price to be averaged from three separate appraisals.

"There was a possibility with that very high initial appraisal, the middle would be much higher than our negotiated price," said Johnson. Thankfully, the other two appraisers were savvy to the distinctions in real estate value between standard commercial property in Oakland County, and this kind of narrow linear parcel that had little potential for any other practical use. The two lower appraisals brought them back to the already agreed-upon price.

The group prepared an application for funding through the Michigan Natural Resources Trust Fund, then known as the Michigan Land Trust Fund.

"I remember going to represent this grant proposal to a meeting of what must've been the Natural Resources Commission. The chairman of that commission was a mighty force in conservation in the

state of Michigan named Tom Washington who had been the director of the Michigan United Conservation Clubs," said Tomboulian. "That was a good piece of luck. It was a little scary to be talking to Tom Washington with our little homemade map of what we wanted to do, but they did approve paying 50 percent—$225,000. So it was at that point going to happen."

On May 26, 1983, the Penn Central Detroit Bay City Branch Line, formerly the Michigan Central Detroit Bay City Branch Line, officially became the Paint Creek Trail and the real work began. The trail was now officially public property, but it was hardly a developed pathway ready for public use. Actual trail design and construction would take years to complete. But some users weren't waiting.

"When we received the trail, it was basically a linear stretch of flattened land with crushed rock. It was a convenient place for people to drive in with trucks and dump trash," Said Tomboulian.

Dirt bikers favored it too, even building moguls to jump along the path. The roar could be heard day and night as they tore up and down the trail, annoying neighbors and reigniting some of the property owners' worst fears.

"We had several cases of off-road vehicles who came on it the years before the trail was developed and opened for use. And there were accidents," said Johnson. "At the south end south of Rochester, the Clinton River had eroded through the railroad bed. One night a couple of Jeeps went roaring down there unaware of this and plunged off into the Clinton River."

The plans included creating artificial barriers for vehicles, but some of the more willful trespassers still managed to go around them.

"We built wooden barricades to stop them, and nearby campers from the state park took down the barricades to build campfires. And then we tried mounds of dirt and the motorcyclists said, 'oh, this is a playground to go over,'" said Johnson. "What really stopped it was we had a resident who owned a gravel pit. He generously donated and delivered some very large boulders to place around the designed barriers that had been circumvented. That really was the end of that."

Local officials worked hard to reassure residents that the right type of trail use would eventually drive out these undesirable uses. But that wouldn't happen until the "real" trail was constructed.

One large point of public discussion was the trail surface itself. Some wanted asphalt pavement while others preferred a more rural and informal crushed limestone surface.

"We knew limestone paving had been used extensively on trails in Wisconsin so we were able to talk about the pros and cons, but largely it was the sentiments expressed at public meetings. The public said don't make the trail look like it's paved for motor vehicles to use."

Even the width of the trail was a point of contention.

"It was built to an eight-foot-wide standard because that was the national standard at that time. Believe it or not, there were people who thought that was too wide, too urban, too much like a highway, and it should be six feet or four feet like a footpath," said Tomboulian. "Well, we had to deal with that. It was unusually wide, it was not a sidewalk. It was a trail that would allow two bicycles in opposite directions to pass each other safely."

The Paint Creek Trailways plan was honored with an award from the Michigan Society of Planning

Officials in 1986. In 1988, an Inland Fisheries grant funded four enhancement projects along the trail. The actual trail surface design began in 1989. In 1990, the Paint Creek Trailways Commission was awarded a Certificate of Merit from the U.S. Department of the Interior.

The trail surface was completed in 1990, and the Oakland County Sheriff's Department began mounted patrols. And sure enough, the walkers and bicyclists began to show up. More, in fact, than anyone had anticipated or hoped.

"Actually, there was a period where there were no other trails in Oakland County, so we had a lot of people flocking here and the trail was getting very crowded," said Johnson. "I have to admit I wanted to see more trails established just so people would stay home and use the trails in their own hometown."

As the trail's popularity grew, the trail commission found itself dealing with a variety of unexpected issues that required the hiring of John Makris, an attorney with extensive experience with railroad corridors.

For example, two historic homes on the far side of the creek had driveways that crossed the path from their Orion Road access.

"I remember going out and sitting down with the landowners and talking very specifically about the potential problems. They were understandably afraid of what would happen if they drove in their driveway and hit a trail user," said Johnson. "We imposed warning signs on both sides of the driveways and also suggested they not go barreling up the driveway at 30 mph. The homeowners did agree and it's worked out well."

A few property owners had long-established fence lines for their horses or cattle that encroached onto the railroad right of way. Makris worked with them on pulling back their fences to avoid obstructing the new pathway.

Now that they saw the trail as a recreational asset, almost every homeowner along the trail wanted to create their own private access directly from their own backyards. In some cases, those improvements were considered potential hazards for trail users, like wooden steps going up a steep bank.

"We ended up making it so that anyone who wanted to create an access had to submit plans to be approved by the Trailways Commission," said Johnson. "We didn't mind them creating the access. We just didn't want them creating things that trail users might trip over if they wandered off the beaten path."

They also had to ease property owners' fears of liability should someone wander onto private property and get injured.

"Michigan had recently passed a recreational user's excuse of liability that had been principally motivated by a need to ensure there was no liability for private property owners if a

The business owners themselves echo the enthusiasm for the trail's economic impact. And interestingly, it isn't just restaurants and ice cream shops that benefit.

canoeist portaged around an obstacle onto their private property. The law also said the recreational user has to use the minimum route required to circumvent the obstacle."

Other issues included dealing with utilities companies for occasional closings along sections of the trail for necessary utilities service work.

"It's all certainly increased interaction between the four local governments," Johnson said. "Historically there'd been some bitter feelings between Rochester and Rochester Hills (formerly Avon Township) over some land acquisition elsewhere. Having to meet and talk with each other on a monthly basis for the trail completely ended that old animosity. In fact, I can remember many of the meetings where the two would get into their own little sub-conversations off on the side, like old friends. The trail was a real vehicle for opening up communications between the communities."

BOOTS, BIKES, AND BUSINESS

In 1996, discussions were launched to extend the trail into Lake Orion. At the time the corridor was purchased, a Lake Orion business near M-24 needed the abutting land for parking, so the trail had to end just outside town. But now a developer was planning a large apartment complex between downtown Lake Orion and the trail. As part of the development, the trail was paved through the complex and on into town.

"As a result, now there's a restaurant in town that we often eat at whenever a group of us ride the Paint Creek Trail," said avid bicyclist Jack Minore, a former state legislator and founding member of the Friends of the Flint River Trail. He has also been a board member of the Michigan Trails & Greenways Alliance for nearly ten years. "We also like to visit two restaurants at the south end. One is a bar with a little deck and takeout window with easy access to the trail. I have been in there many times on a Saturday afternoon when a bar is normally empty and there'll be six tables of bicyclists there eating burgers and sandwiches. A little pizza shop across the creek also does a fair business on bicyclists. And anywhere there's an ice cream shop, I can guarantee you'll find us."

"Downtown Lake Orion is very fortunate to be connected to the Paint Creek Trail. Our residents enjoy the healthy living amenities of the trail including opportunities to enjoy nature, connect to other communities, and experience all the benefits of a walkable community," said Lake Orion DDA Executive Director Suzanne Perreault. "In addition, many of our businesses have benefited from the foot and bike traffic as well."

The business owners themselves echo the enthusiasm for the trail's economic impact. And interestingly, it isn't just restaurants and ice cream shops that benefit.

"The Paint Creek Trail has been fabulous for downtown Lake Orion. I have been opened for almost eight years and have noticed more and more walkers and riders on a daily basis. Most come with backpacks for purchases, or buy and then leave their purchases with us to only come back later for pickup," said Kristy Kowatch, owner of Twice Blessed Children's and Divas Women Consignment. "What's really neat is that it's such a testimony for other shoppers in our stores and on the sidewalks. Conversations come up all the time and others join in the delight of the trails."

"We are looking forward to the warm weather again and bike riders to come and visit us. I'm amazed, especially on Saturdays, the number of bicyclists that travel from Rochester to Lake Orion to dine and shop," said Beth Lofay, co-owner of Simply Marcella. "We've had to make special arrangements for our guests who have had so much fun shopping and can't fit their purchases on their bikes. Such a great problem! We are so grateful to the bikers who visit Lake Orion."

Johnson said that a number of businesses were created specifically to cater to trail users in the communities along the trail.

"The business community has really benefitted. There are bike shops now and new restaurants. Plus some of the older ones started getting a lot of new business so they helped in establishing bike racks and facilities and making contributions to the trail," said Johnson. "In fact, a very expensive hotel was built in downtown Rochester abutting the trail and Paint Creek where they have bike racks and an outdoor deck where you can eat lunch. They even have bikes that hotel guests can use free of charge."

Even the old Paint Creek Cider Mill has gotten a new lease on life—literally. Situated on Orion Road on the bank of the Paint Creek in Oakland Township just north of Rochester, the original mill was built in 1835 by Needham Hemingway, one of the first settlers in this area. In 1836, Hemingway hand-dug the mill race to supply water power for his gristmill, a key factor contributing to the settlement of the community which became known as Goodison in 1872. Although the water power from the mill race was used to generate electricity up until 1998, the building itself was dismantled in about 1955. Reconstruction began in 1959 or 1960 and was completed in 1973, according to Barbara Barber, historic preservation planner for Oakland Township's Historic District Commission. For the next 20 plus years, the mill operated a cider mill and restaurant serving fresh, pressed cider, produced onsite. After sitting vacant for a number of years, the building was donated in 2005 to Oakland Township by its then-current owners, Mr. and Mrs. Ray Nicholson. The township converted the upstairs of the building into offices for the Oakland Township Parks and Recreation Department, as well as three other public entities. The downstairs restaurant area was converted into a community meeting room.

Restoration of the building, including adaptive use improvements for the upstairs office, was completed by preservation architect John Dziurman. In the fall of 2008, the Parks and Recreation, Historic District Commission, Paint Creek Trailways Commission, and Six Rivers Land Conservancy moved upstairs to the second floor office space. Several tenants have leased the restaurant space since 2008. The current tenant is local businessman Ed Granchi who came in 2012, and is the first to remain open year-round.

Granchi leases the former cider sales area in the downstairs of the building where he operates a small restaurant called the Paint Creek Cider Mill. In little more than a year and a half, he has made his restaurant into a positive part of the community, and his clientele has been steadily growing. Meyers said it has become a favorite spot for trail users to grab a lunch or sit in the shade with a hand-scooped ice cream cone on a sunny afternoon.

"My background has been in restaurant operation for many years prior to the Paint Creek Cider Mill. I thought it would be a great place to expand on what was already happening," said Granchi. "I also grew up coming to the Paint Creek Cider Mill as a child. I even

have hanging in the dining room a picture of my mother holding me when I was one year old in front of the water wheel."

Granchi has even brought the historic mill back to its roots.

"The previous owner had a concession menu in place and was making donuts and buying other cider and then reselling it to patrons. I saw so much potential for the location and what a cider mill should offer. A cider mill to me meant down-home, hand-crafted, small-batch comfort food," said Granchi. "So I decided to bring back cider pressing to the building. I believe it had been about 15 years since anyone had pressed cider on location, and it went on from there. I created a much larger comprehensive menu of some family recipes of mine and had lots of fun incorporating apples or cider into much of the menu, from the house cider BBQ sauce to the from-scratch baked beans."

Granchi said that business has been booming, mostly thanks to simple word of mouth—and nose.

"Having the cider mill and café business on the Paint Creek Trail has been a great pairing. It falls almost at the midway point of the trail, an easy ride with the family either from downtown Rochester or downtown Lake Orion. The Paint Creek Cider Mill has become more than just a restroom stop, or a place to rest the legs," said Granchi.

"On the weekends, the wafting aromas of hardwood smoked meats can be enjoyed when approaching the cider mill

on the trail, and I have had many people say they weren't even hungry until they got close. Then they are even more pleasantly surprised to find that I have started to press cider again, and how big the menu is. Or they have heard how good the pizza is, or that they can taste old-time homemade draft root beer. With our large parking lot, trail riders also find it ideal to meet here and go out for a ride and rendezvous back here to have some lunch on the gorgeous brick paver patio."

The mill race was awarded a Michigan State Historic Marker in 2002, and the Historic District Commission is currently working to have the mill building listed on the National Register of Historic Places to honor our local heritage, said Barber.

Meanwhile, the trail's economic impact continues to grow. The Paint Creek Crawl is an annual event designed to bring trail users into the communities and businesses along the trail.

"For the 4th Annual Paint Creek Crawl on June 7, we are going to headquarter at Children's Park in downtown Lake Orion, and try to shed some light on the great businesses downtown that can be accessed by taking the trail," said Kristen Myers, trail manager for the Paint Creek Trailways Commission. "The past three years, our Crawl event has brought 150 cyclists into both downtown Rochester and downtown Lake Orion to many stores. Riders had to take the trail to both downtowns, ride to particular businesses, and get a stamp in a 'passport.' Many riders commented how great it was to learn about businesses that were so close to the trail. I'm sure the businesses got a boost in traffic from it."

The clever concept is an ideal venue for businesses that might not ordinarily attract trail users in the course of a regular recreational outing.

"We like the bikers, they stop by and then drive back to pick up various items. We also participate in the (Paint Creek Crawl) bike run every spring as a stamp station and we try to give them a free gift," said Lloyd Coe of Ed's Broadway Gifts & Costumes in Lake Orion. "It creates goodwill and is loads of fun."

In fact, trail events have become so popular the Commission has had to restrict the number of them allowed.

"We had so many nonprofits that wanted to hold fundraisers on the trail, we were starting to get complaints from residents that they couldn't enjoy the trail on the weekends. So now we've limited the number to maybe one a month," said Johnson.

Back before the trail was built, many homeowners worried the trail's proximity would bring down their property values. The exact opposite has happened.

"Although I don't have hard data regarding rising property values, I can tell you that in the past, realtors have told me that homes near the trail had a 20 percent increase in property values compared to similar houses that were not on the trail," said Myers.

"In fact, property owners selling homes have sometimes tried sneaking 'for sale' signs up along the trail itself—an understandable temptation but one that's absolutely prohibited," Johnson said.

"But you can hardly blame them for trying," she said, chuckling. "We've had real estate agents tell us they have people looking to buy a home and the first thing they ask is if they have any available abutting or very close to the trail."

In the years since, the Paint Creek Trail has become part of an ever-growing trail network that is linking up all across Oakland County and southeast

Michigan. The Grand Trunk tracks in northeast Shelby Township have been removed and converted into the Macomb Orchard Trail, a 24-mile linear park that starts at 24 Mile Road and Dequindre in Shelby Township and travels northeast to the city of Richmond.[5] The Macomb Orchard connects to the Clinton River Trail near the south end of the Paint Creek Trail. The Clinton River Trail is a 16-mile east-west route crossing through the communities of Sylvan Lake, Pontiac, Auburn Hills, Rochester Hills, and the city of Rochester.[6]

The trail network begun by the pioneers of Paint Creek now connects 180 miles of completed or planned trails in southeast Michigan.

"How do I feel about what we've accomplished? Remember, our family was enjoying this as a trail back when it was still operated as a railroad and wasn't even supposed to be a trail at all," said Johnson, laughing. "It's personally very satisfying to know that so many people will continue to enjoy all this for many years to come."

(ENDNOTES)

1 "Michigan Trail Facts," Michigan Trails and Greenways Alliance, accessed February 13, 2014, http://michigantrails.org/newsroom.

2 "Central Michigan Railroads," Wikipedia, accessed February 18, 2014, http://www.shiawasseehistory.com/cmrr.html.

3 Leslie E. Arndt, "The Bay County Story – Memoirs of the County's 125 Years" Huron News Service, 1982, "Footpaths to Freeways" pp. 210, accessed February 18, 2014, http://bay-journal.com/bay/1he/writings/rr-memory-campbell-harriet.html.

4 "Paint Creek Trail – Connecting Our Communities Since 1983," Paint Creek Trailways Commission, accessed February 18, 2014, http://www.paintcreektrail.org/.

5 "Macomb Orchard Trail," Macomb County, Michigan, accessed March 7, 2014, http://www.macombcountymi.gov/macomborchardtrail/index.htm.

6 Friends of the Clinton River Trail, accessed March 7, 2014, http://www.clintonrivertrail.org/.

CASE STUDY

Noquemanon Trails Network

Marquette, Michigan — Pop. 21,355

PROJECT SCOPE

How do you leverage a recreational facility to turn your city into a national recreational tourism destination? The Noquemanon Trails Network (NTN), in the north-central region of Michigan's Upper Peninsula (U.P.), was enhanced to cater to off-road bicyclists, expanding the recreational tourism brand of the area and establishing the city of Marquette as a national destination for cyclists—yielding impressive economic results for the private sector.

The terrain and extreme seasons of Marquette lend it to a four-season silent sports activity[1] that has historically been part of the local culture. The Noquemanon Trails Network is a 501c3 that emerged from an unofficial volunteer group concerned with maintaining trails when state resources became untenable about 10 years ago. At the same time, the city of Marquette was actively repositioning itself from a former industrial community to a premiere recreational tourism destination. In this pursuit, the city purchased 2,243 acres in the city and contiguous townships, enabling expansion of NTN's silent sports trail system within city boundaries and beyond. Unanimously approved by city officials, the acquisition was dubbed the "Louisiana Purchase" for its future economic importance.

While the city invested in strategic land purchases and connecting trails to the downtown, NTN took up the challenge of major trail development and maintenance. NTN proceeded with the goals of erosion control, preservation, and an excellent trail experience for all skill levels, multiple generations, and all user types. With this investment, mountain bike (Singletrack) use exploded, and Marquette is now a national year-round silent sports destination. The city, Downtown Development Authority (DDA), and Convention and Visitors Bureau (CVB) all play a role in promoting this brand and attracting visitors. NTN's focus is changing from infrastructure development to events, many of which are coordinated with the city's downtown interests. The city will soon develop high-end condominium units in the popular Heartwood area providing immediate trail access for residents, and additional tax base for the community.

INVESTMENT

>> The city of Marquette purchased 2,243 acres to expand the trail system.

>> Private donations, memberships, and events support ongoing maintenance and development.

>> The Noquemanon Trails Network is a 501c3 dedicated to developing, maintaining, signing, and mapping a non-motorized land and water trail network throughout Marquette and Alger Counties in Michigan's Upper Peninsula. The network—used for hiking, running, off-road biking, horseback riding, skiing, snowshoeing, canoeing, and kayaking—is vital to Marquette's success as a premiere destination for recreational tourism.

>> NTN has a 17-member board of volunteers, representing all user interests. Several members of the board are both trail users and local business owners with a vested interest in the success of the trails and promotion of the area as a recreational tourism destination. NTN has one full-time director and hires some part-time trail builders and maintenance workers, however, most maintenance is accomplished through volunteers.

SOCIOECONOMIC IMPACT

>> Increased annual hotel sales by 25,000 rooms from 2009–2012, primarily through two major recreational events. A conservative estimate of an additional $150 spent on the local economy per room sold, equals nearly $3.8 million, not including spending estimates of local/regional participants and spectators.

>> Created the stimulus, through development of downtown trail access, for more than $40 million in private investment and provided the impetus for more than $12 million in other public projects. New businesses include two brew pubs representing $750,000 of investment and 14 employees; seven restaurants representing $2 million of investment and 80 employees; as well as other new and expanded shops and businesses. The taxable value of downtown properties is up 83 percent, with new downtown residential increasing 200 percent (townhouse, condo and second-story residential).

>> Doubled the number of major trail event participants annually and created a year-round recreation destination by welcoming and investing in Singletrack users.

>> Attracts Singletrack users from across the Midwest and Canada throughout the season (not just for events), as evidenced by license plates at trailheads.

>> Launched an annual Noquemanon Ski Marathon, which is part of the American Ski Marathon Series and is an FIS (International Ski Federation) points race.

The race draws Olympic competitors, has reached its maximum capacity of 1,400 participants, and is enjoyed by countless spectators. Six hundred volunteers work the event which includes: marathon and half-marathon, 12K, youth races, snowshoeing, skijor (skiers pulled by dogs or horses), snow-biking, and sit ski (adaptive skiing for the physically challenged) events. Annual NTN skiers and snowshoers are estimated at 28,000.

>> Launched Ore to Shore Mountain Bike Epic, drawing 2,387 participants in 2012, attracting national cycling team participation and creating additional exposure for Marquette as a premiere cycling destination. Four hundred volunteers work the event, which included 48-mile, 28-mile, and 10-mile races with various youth events. The Ore to Shore cycling route incorporates downtown Marquette.

>> Launched first Fat Tire (snow bike) Winter Event as part of Ski Marathon events in 2013.

>> Utilized the International Mountain Biking Association (IMBA) to train Marquette stakeholders in becoming an IMBA-recognized destination. In this pursuit, NTN hired a master trail builder to create trails for all skill levels that also include erosion control, engineered to coexist with the environment. Once IMBA recognition is achieved, NTN will receive national exposure to 35,000 IMBA members and retailers.

>> Inspired DDA/city to plan ambitious recreational events downtown.

>> The new 2012 summer Bike Jam combined NTN Single Track trail events with downtown bike events, appealing to all skill levels, bike types, and families.

>> The new 2013 winter Rail Jam is a downtown event for snowboard competitors, promoted in conjunction with the U.P. 200 Sled Dog event (an Iditarod qualifying race).

>> Inspired DDA/city to brand for recreational tourists: high profile bike racks in downtown create a welcoming bike culture and promote Marquette's many other recreational tourism attractions such as hockey, music, freighter watching, etc.

>> Inspired Marquette General Hospital and other major employers to use the NTN system as a quality of life recruitment tool.

>> Attracted major players in bike industry to test ride new bike lines on NTN trails.

>> Attracted skijors and sit skiers.

LESSONS LEARNED

>> Recognize widespread popularity of canine companions and designated canine-friendly trails.

>> Separate trail users by activity (to degree possible) to maximize trail experience for all.

>> Recognize an abundance of natural and social capital is what makes this endeavor successful. The energy and desire of sports enthusiasts, coupled with community pride, make for great volunteers.

>> Build a foundation of community pride and celebrate success. The city's adherence to a long-term master plan to reinvent itself from an industrial-based to a recreation/tourism-based community through steady implementation and publicized successes, has fostered community pride and created an enthusiastic resident fan base.

>> Nurture social capital and recruit the active. As a recreation destination with a university and major health industry, Marquette has physically active residents who tend to be high energy and socially connected via their sports networks. Combined with a foundation of community pride, this provides Marquette with effective, reliable volunteer groups and a strong donor base. The city further fosters this culture with numerous citizen boards and committees.

>> Connect the pieces and complement, rather than compete. Marquette's reinvention began as a tourism destination, but simultaneously the city seized opportunities to actively promote and develop its recreation options, providing more pieces of a greater experience. Also, as NTN developed, it chose to complement (rather than compete with) the Keweenaw Peninsula's elite mountain biking destination by positioning itself as a destination for all skill levels, thus creating a regional destination from one area.

>> Seek professional help. As NTN developed single-track, it sought expert guidance from the International Mountain Biking Association on becoming an IMBA destination, thus developing an appeal to all skill levels, including youth, and hiring a master trail builder to engineer erosion control to coexist with the environment.

>> Build on Success. Don't expect instant success, but recognize potential. Try new things and shake it up to see what works (or doesn't). The annual Ski Marathon, limited to 1,400 participants, grew from a smaller event which drew a few hundred skiers. The Ski Marathon now offers a Fat Tire (bicycling) event in recognition of the growing cyclist base, and inspired the first annual 2013 Rail Jam snowboard competition. The Ore-to-Shore bike event, which draws more than 2,300 participants, inspired the 2012 first annual Bike Jam.

>> Be Authentic. The natural assets and terrain lent itself as the perfect backdrop for careful development as a recreation destination for silent sports. A long history of outdoor sports was further cultivated, and students from Northern Michigan University, as well as local business owners, introduced new and creative activities, such as skijoring, which keeps the excitement high. Other

communities may have different recreational assets to develop. Grow what you know.

>> Collect the Data. Marketing decisions are based on participant data regarding local, out-of-area, out-of-state, or international participants. The CVB reports steady annual growth in hotel rooms sold from 2008–2012, now up more than 25,000 rooms annually. Further, a conservative estimate of $150 spent on the local economy per room sold yields a $4 million increase from 2009. These figures do not reflect regional participants and spectators.

>> Adjust the Lens. As NTN's trails developed and popularity grew, NTN's focus changed from being primarily an infrastructure-based organization to an events-based organization. Events are used as significant fundraisers to complement donor and membership dollars, while simultaneously creating buzz and feeding the media, serving to further market and promote the trails.

>> Bam! The original trail users were primarily local and singularly focused on recreation, never dreaming that what they created would have such a stunning impact on both the image and the economy of an entire city. Fortunately, the city, DDA, and CVB all recognized NTN's growing contribution to the health of the community and are able to collaborate on events and capitalize on this enormous asset.

>> Growing Pains. Accept these as healthy; the alternative is stagnation or decline. Deliberately plan to manage change. NTN experienced significant controversy over how much of NTN resources from a loyal skier base to devote to Singletrack. At this point, it's a full embrace.

>> Recognize Opportunity. Seize the day, but work diligently to manage outcomes by getting the right people at the table working in an atmosphere of respect, while fostering cooperation and minimizing emotion. The pursuit of opportunity sometimes results in others being stepped on, so minimize the pain.

>> Breaking Up Is Hard to Do. At some point, a parting of the ways may be unavoidable. For example, the Superiorland Cross Country Ski Club separated itself from NTN in 2011 to focus on their niche of youth programming. As much as possible, hold original interests harmless and move forward, remaining open to a new type of relationship with former partners.

>> Partner Smart. In Marquette, recreational development was the goal of the users, prior to its economic impact. Other communities may partner effectively from the beginning with economic impact as the primary goal, recognizing authentic recreation development as a means to achieving this.

(ENDNOTES)

1 "Silent Sports," Silent Sports magazine, accessed May 30, 2014, http://www.silentsports.net.

Moving Placemaking Forward Through Bike Trails

• Michigan took a giant step forward in 2010 by enacting Complete Streets legislation calling for roadways designed to be accessible for all legal users including cars, trucks, mass transit, wheelchair users, bicyclists, and pedestrians. Many communities are starting to pass local ordinances and implement plans to incorporate Complete Streets concepts into their roadways. "A Citizen's Guide to Promoting Complete Streets" is available on the Michigan State University Extension website.[1]

• Trail Town Initiatives: One could indeed simply "build it and they will come." But a growing body of evidence shows that in order to maximize a trail's full economic potential, it should be part of a comprehensive placemaking strategy. This is coming to be known nationally as the Trail Town concept. Specific components of the Trail Town concept include downtown design guidelines, walkability tactics, and promotional strategies that all work together to create a Trail Town. In 2013, the Kentucky Office for Adventure Tourism established a Trail Towns Program to promote and develop adventure tourism opportunities along the state's extensive trail networks and wild rivers. Kentucky's first Trail Town was designated in May and more than 30 communities have started the application process to become an official Kentucky Trail Town. Here in Michigan, the North Country Trail Association recently established a Trail Town Program with help from the National Parks System. As of December 2013, three Michigan communities (St. Ignace, Mackinaw City, and Petoskey) had already been awarded Trail Town status, with Kalkaska in the approval process.[2]

Trail towns can also be based around waterways and other types of trails. In southern Michigan, the Clinton River Watershed Council and the Huron River Watershed recently launched their own Trail Town Programs for water-oriented community development.

• Founded in 1993, the Land Information Access Association (LIAA) is a nonprofit service organization that helps people cooperatively plan for, preserve, and manage the unique cultural and natural resources required for sustainable, resilient communities. LIAA has been involved in over a dozen local Trail Town initiatives and many trail planning projects all over Michigan.

• "Trail Towns – Capturing Trail-Based Tourism: A Manual for Communities in Northern Michigan" was prepared by LIAA for the UpNorth Trails Initiative with funding provided by Pure Michigan. The complete manual can be found online at the LIAA website (www.liaa.org) under the Services tab for Parks, Recreation and Trails. The following is an excerpt:

A Trail Town is a community in which local officials have used their trail system as the focal point of a tourism-centered strategy for economic development and local revitalization. The Trail Town concept was originally developed by the Allegheny Trail Alliance, a coalition of seven trail organizations along the Great Allegheny Passage, a 150-mile multi-use trail running through Pennsylvania and Maryland. Many communities in Michigan are now working to develop their own local Trail Town Program. The basic Trail Town concept is simple: ensure that communities along the trail are better able to maximize the economic potential of trail-based tourism.

The local Trail Town effort can be centered around any type of trail (e.g., non-motorized, snow-mobile, equestrian, and kayak). While the Trail Town concept is primarily geared toward cities and towns, the concept is very much applicable in rural areas that have at least one small center of commercial activity. Most Trail towns are not isolated communities—they are linked together by the trail, creating a regional destination for residents, trail users, and tourists.

HOW DOES A COMMUNITY ESTABLISH A TRAIL TOWN?

While there are a number of different ways in which local communities can organize around an effort to create a Trail Town Program, the most common approach has been to use the "Four Point Approach®" developed by the National Main Street Center of the National Trust for Historic Preservation.

1. Organization. Establishes consensus and cooperation by building partnerships among various groups that have a stake in the local trail system and the downtown.

2. Promotion. Sells the image and promise of a Trail Town to all prospects.

3. Design. Gets the Trail Town into top physical shape to create a safe and appealing environment.

4. Economic Restructuring. Helps existing businesses expand and recruit new businesses to respond to current trail activities and market forces.

WHAT ARE THE BENEFITS OF BECOMING A TRAIL TOWN?

Over the last several years, as the full economic potential of linking trails, recreation, tourism and business development has become better known, the Trail Town concept has caught on. According to an article from the Rails-to-Trails Conservancy, "communities around the country are increasingly utilizing the 'trail town' model of economic revitalization that places trails as the centerpiece of a tourism-centered strategy for small town revitalization." In fact, studies from neighboring states like Wisconsin have shown that bicycle tourism supports more than $900 million in tourism and residential spending each year.[3]

• Public funding for bike trails and other community and economic development initiatives can often be secured from local, state, and federal government programs. These financial aid programs may include Michigan Trust Fund grants from the Michigan Department of Natural Resources, enhancement grants from the Michigan Department of Transportation, and development grants from the Coastal Zone Management Program, Michigan Economic Development Corporation, the U.S. Department of Agriculture, and others.

• Local foundations, trail and recreation advocacy organizations, and local conservation groups are a valuable source of funding for trail initiatives and ongoing support. Local leaders or a professional grant writer can be helpful in researching and writing grants on behalf of the Trail Town initiative and local communities. Organizations like the Northern Lakes Economic Alliance (serving northern Michigan), the regional Councils of Government, and the Michigan Municipal League can be very helpful in identifying such grant opportunities.

• A Recreation Authority property tax millage can be used to finance the construction and maintenance of pathways and/or acquire property. The Recreational Authority Act 321 of 2000 authorizes a Recreational Authority to levy a tax of not more than 1 mill for a period of not more than 20 years on all of the taxable property within the territory of the authority. A Recreation Authority may be a good option for communities in which the trail passes through neighboring jurisdictions.

• Local funding tools like Tax Increment Financing (TIF) can help finance the public costs associated with development and redevelopment projects. The local government freezes the tax base within a specific development district and uses the revenues generated by reassessment or new development to finance selected improvements within the district. The term "tax increment" refers to the additional taxes resulting from private development that are earmarked or "captured" for the TIF Authority's use for public improvements, which are then financed either on a pay-as-you-go basis from the annual tax increment revenues, or the municipality may issue tax increment bonds to finance public improvements and use the annual tax increment revenues to retire the bond.[4]

• The Corridor Improvement Authority (CIA) Public Act 280 of 2005 is designed to assist communities with funding improvements in commercial corridors outside of their main commercial or downtown areas. Any city, village, or township may establish an authority. While the CIA program is similar in nature to a Downtown Development Authority, there are distinct differences that make the CIA uniquely suited to "trail town" projects. For example, more than one authority is permitted within a municipality, and a Corridor Improvement Authority may enter into inter-local agreements with adjoining municipalities. Once created, a Corridor Improvement Authority may hire a director, establish a tax increment financing plan, levy special assessments, and issue revenue bonds and notes.[5]

• The Rails-to-Trails Conservancy (RTC) is a 501c3 nonprofit organization "dedicated to creating a nationwide network of trails from former rail lines and connecting corridors to build healthier places for healthier people."[6] The headquarters is located in Washington, D.C., with field and regional offices in Ohio, Pennsylvania, California, and Florida. More information can be found at www.railstotrails.org and www.traillink.com.

• According to RTC President Keith Laughlin, more than 21,000 miles of unused rail corridor have been converted to non-motorized trails, preserving almost one quarter of all rail corridor that has fallen into disuse since the 1950s, with more than 7,000 miles of new rail-trail projects currently underway. At the same time, the U.S. railroad industry appears to have stabilized, with only about 6,000 miles of additional track abandoned between 2000 and 2011. In response, the RTC is now increasing emphasis on rails-with-trails projects. According to a recent RTC report, there are currently 188 trails in 42 states that include mileage along active trail lines.[7]

• The Michigan Trails & Greenways Alliance (MTGA) (www.MichiganTrails.org) is a 501c3 nonprofit membership organization that helps create, advocate, and connect trails across Michigan. A former field office of the Rails-to-Trails Conservancy, the MTGA, is now solely focused in Michigan. The group can assist local trail building efforts with presentations, trail literature distribution, and various types of interaction and collaboration.

• The League of American Bicyclists (LAB) (www.bikeleague.org) and its state chapters, such as the League of Michigan Bicyclists (LMB), work to promote bicycling and bike safety, and also advocate at the local, state, and national level for bicycle-related legislation, education, and public policies. Here are some of the recommendations from LAB and LMB to increase bikeability:[8]

1. Adopt a safe passing law with a minimum distance of three feet to address bicyclist safety.

2. Adopt a vulnerable road user law that increases penalties for a motorist that injures or kills a bicyclist or pedestrian.

3. Adopt a statewide, all-ages cell phone ban to combat distracted driving and increase safety for everyone.

4. Adopt performance measures, such as mode shift or a low percentage of exempted projects, to better track and support Complete Streets/Bike Accommodation Policy compliance.

5. Adopt a policy requiring state office buildings, state park and recreation facilities, and other state facilities to provide bicycle parking.

6.Since arterial and collector roads are the backbone of every transportation network, it is essential to provide adequate bicycle facilities along these roads.

7. Hold a bicycle ride sponsored by the governor and/or legislators to show their constituents that their elected officials support bicycling.

8. Adopt a statewide bicycle plan with clear implementation actions and performance measures to gauge success.

9. Adopt a mode share goal for biking to encourage the integration of bicycle transportation needs into all transportation and land use policy and project decisions.

10. Ensure that bicycle safety is a major emphasis in all transportation projects, programs, and policies to address this issue.

(ENDNOTES)

1 "A Citizens Guide to Promoting Complete Streets," Michigan State University Extension, June 12, 2013, accessed May 30, 2014, http://msue.anr.msu.edu/news/a_citizens_guide_to_promoting_complete_streets.

2 "Trail Towns – Capturing Trial-Based Tourism: A Manual for Communities in Northern Michigan," Land Information Access Association, December 2013, accessed February 21, 2014, http://www.liaa.org/downloads/trail_town_manual_1.pdf.

3 Ibid.

4 MSPO *Community Planning Handbook*, excerpt, Tax Increment Financing, Michigan Association of Planning, accessed February 21, 2014, http://www.planningmi.org/downloads/tax_increment_financing.pdf.

5 "Economic Development Tools – Corridor Improvement Authority, One Pager Plus," Michigan Municipal League, July 2008, http://www.mml.org/pdf/opp/opp_cia.pdf.

6 Editorial masthead, *Rails to Trails Magazine*, Spring/Summer 2014, 2.

7 Keith Laughlin, "Expanding Our Bag of Tricks," *Rails to Trails Magazine*, Spring/Summer 2014, 2.

8 "Report Cards," The League of American Bicyclists, accessed May 31, 2014, http://bikeleague.org/content/report-cards.

What if you threw a party and nobody came?

Sadly, that's what can happen when a community neglects to make its citizens a part of the process. Whether it's seeking a millage to build a new park or tackling neighborhood crime, if the people aren't involved, the effort is doomed regardless of local leaders' good intentions.

But when local government acts as the host of the party—and then gets out of the way—there's no limit to what the "power of the people" can accomplish in surprisingly new and creative ways.

During his 2011 TEDxIowaCity presentation "For the Love of Cities," national community development expert Peter Kageyama had this to say about successful grassroots engagement efforts: "They start with people who are emotionally engaged with their city, people who love their city, and who want to do something above and beyond ordinary citizenship, and maybe do something extraordinary for their city. We like to think that's a fairly common notion, but it turns out it's actually not."[1]

Kageyama backs that up with findings from the 2008–2010 Gallup "Soul of the Community" survey for the Knight Foundation, which found that 40 percent of those surveyed felt unattached to their home city, and another 36 percent felt neutral. Less than a quarter said they felt attached to their city.

At the same time, Gallup's economic data showed that those cities with the highest levels of emotional engagement, passion, and loyalty were also the cities with the highest levels of local GDP and economic vitality.

That might not be a causal relationship, says Kageyama, but it's something worth noting. "When children are loved, they thrive. So too with plants, pets, and objects," said Kageyama. "Don't you think if we invested more of our love and our identity and our emotional side into our communities, then they would not shine like that car? I believe they would."

(ENDNOTES)

1 Peter Kageyama, "TEDx Iowa City – Peter Kageyama – For the Love of Cities," YouTube, uploaded November 30, 2011, accessed March 13, 2014, http://www.youtube.com/watch?v=6k7OKw_rSz0.

CIVIC ENGAGEMENT

DETROIT CITY FUTBOL LEAGUE

Rebuilding Neighborhoods
On The Soccer Field

Back in 2008, despite their best efforts, Sean Mann and his neighbors were just another group of Detroiters frustrated at the blight and crime in their inner city neighborhood, and looking for a new way to confront it.

They were a mix of both newcomers and longtime residents, young and old, living in a typical middle class neighborhood in southwest Detroit. They weren't trying to change the world. They just wanted to make some kind of positive impact on the community in which they lived.

"We were building upon the efforts of residents from previous generations. We just took a different approach," said Mann. "One of my mentors in the neighborhood organized picnics in Clark Park in the 1980s during a much rougher stretch than I've ever seen, trying to take back the park and make it a place that families utilized. Stuff like that inspired me to live in the neighborhood in the first place."

Mann had the perfect background to be part of a "different approach." Just a few years before, Mann had returned to Michigan after living abroad in England where he did postgraduate study in international relations and worked at the House of Commons. Upon his return, he began advocating in Lansing to promote positive physical changes in Michigan's distressed cities and urban areas, and helped launch Let's Save Michigan, a citizen

engagement and advocacy organization led by the Michigan Municipal League to promote initiatives that encourage the creation of vibrant cities.

That need was obvious in southwest Detroit's historic Hubbard Farms neighborhood, where Mann had recently bought a home.

At the turn of the 19th century, Hubbard Farms was one of the city's most elegant and architecturally impressive neighborhoods, home to doctors, educators, accountants, business owners, and other members of the well-to-do professional class. Over the next few decades, the area grew increasingly diverse as waves of new immigrants flocked to Detroit from various parts of the world, adding a new flavor and vibrancy to its social life and businesses.[1]

But by the late 20th century, Hubbard Farms was struggling against the same economic decline and demographic trends that had beset the rest of the city. Still, much of the unique housing stock from the 1880s to 1920s remained mostly intact in a fairly stable neighborhood with a decades-long reputation for its core group of very active and engaged citizens. By the early 2000s, it had become a magnet for the new breed of urbanists who were moving into Detroit and other distressed urban areas across the country.

Like many of them, Mann saw the potential and was passionate about helping to revitalize his adopted neighborhood. He volunteered his time and expertise to the Clark Park Coalition, a partner of the Detroit Recreational Department which provides recreational, educational, social, and mentoring programs for southwest Detroit families.

But Mann's Hubbard Farms neighbors knew they needed to do more to hold their ground against the continuing of urban decay. The foreclosure crisis looked like a critical tipping point for the neighborhood. Several of the historic homes had been vacated and were at high risk. He joined with other residents to resurrect their own version of the local block club, taking it upon themselves to board up the vacant houses and clean up blight.

"Once houses get broken into by the scrappers, there's a natural cycle of decline," said Mann. "So a group of younger, established residents formed crews to regularly secure the blighted properties in the community."

Many of them were artists who wanted to promote that as an aspect of the neighborhood's eclectic character. So the club created its own neighborhood "tag": a simple graffiti-like graphic of blue skies and white clouds. The tag began showing up all over Hubbard Farms—on the plywood covering broken windows in vacant houses, and painted over graffiti on overpasses and railroad viaducts.

"It symbolized that the neighbors did this, the neighbors care about this. It was a branding exercise for the neighborhood," said Mann.

Over time, the group's efforts became more ambitious and sophisticated, even carrying out nuisance abatement lawsuits against negligent property owners in the neighborhood. But all the effort began to take a toll.

"It was very taxing on us and our time. The problem is you get burned out getting people to come to do this, to paint over graffiti, remove tags. Especially with the nuisance abatement lawsuits, we found it's hard for community groups to have the necessary

number of people engaged to follow through," said Mann. "These projects that are entirely volunteer driven run out of steam over the long haul with not enough people involved and not enough leaders. Our group became smaller over time, people were becoming less engaged, while others were moving out of the neighborhood."

"So how do you engage other people who might not see the inherent joy in boarding up houses over the weekend? We wanted to think up a more social, fun, and lighthearted tool to engage our neighbors, especially new members of the community."

A BEAUTIFUL GAME

Inspiration came from Mann's years living in England. While there, he had developed a passion for soccer, which most of the world calls football. Like American football, British soccer fans are fiercely loyal to big-name professional teams. But the Brits' love for the "beautiful game" had begun a century earlier with neighborhood football clubs. The hyper-local football leagues were a potent source of community identity and pride.

Could the same thing happen in Detroit?

They decided to form a recreational adult co-ed soccer league, and called it the Detroit City Futbol League (DCFL). Mann became its founder and commissioner.

"We chose soccer because it's a very accessible sport. You don't have to be able to throw

"But that low-budget, no-frills, genuine kind of approach is what made it so endearing and also brought down the level of engagement so it was more about community, and building neighborhoods, not soccer."

anything. You basically just have to be able to walk or run and make contact with the ball with your foot," said Mann. "We established a very relaxed attitude in the beginning to attract people of all skill levels because the point of the league was to bring together neighbors in a fun manner, not to be a competitive soccer league."

In order to recruit players, they began a grassroots marketing campaign with posters proclaiming "Represent Your 'Hood'. Teams forming right now for May 2010," and hung them up all over the city's neighborhoods.

They also began a strategic outreach campaign to community leaders, networking outward from key focal points.

"People put it out on listservs around the community. We knew there were enough people in my neighborhood to get at least two teams. But to get bigger, we started identifying social connectors who knew other people who knew different connectors within the community to get the word out and be advocates for it."

By May of 2010, they had recruited 300 participants from 11 different neighborhoods. The first year's budget was less than $1,000.

"Our goal posts were made of PVC pipe that I'd assemble and disassemble after every game. I was driving around town in my Chrysler Sebring with twenty-some PVC pipes hanging out," said Mann, chuckling. "They were duct-taped in place so if the ball ever struck the goal post, we'd have to take a break in the game to put the goal posts back together.

"But that low-budget, no-frills, genuine kind of approach is what made it so endearing and also brought down the level of engagement so it was more about community, and building neighborhoods, not soccer."

Another key objective was to consciously market the neighborhoods that make up Detroit: familiar names that had lost their luster, like Cass Corridor, Hubbard Farms, Hamtramck, and Woodbridge.

"Like most kids who grew up in Michigan and graduated from college in the late 1990s and early 2000s, the vast majority of my classmates had moved out of the state as quickly as possible. So I came home and found most of my friends had left, and the few who had stayed were not that familiar with Detroit. They were more familiar with Chicago, Brooklyn, and other cities, and the neighborhoods that make up those cities because they've gone there and visited friends here," said Mann. "A city is only as strong as the neighborhoods that make it up. So this was not just about bringing neighbors together in new ways. It was also a branding exercise, a way to promote the neighborhoods that make up the city."

It wasn't about creating new identities. It was about rediscovering what was already there.

"We were building on existing brands. For our neighborhood's team, it's very political. We live right next to the Ambassador Bridge, whose private owner has a very contentious relationship with the neighborhood. So our logo is a fist holding a crushed bridge. It's our protest sign," said Mann. "There are probably three dozen neighbors who've made it their own who've never set foot on the soccer field."

Other neighborhoods followed suit, each creating their own logo with its own unique branding characteristics. The iconic image of the long-abandoned Michigan Central train station is emblazoned beneath the words "Roosevelt United." An elegant wrought iron gate signifies the old Victorian neighborhood of Brush Park.

COMMUNITY BUILDING

From the very beginning, the focus was on community, not recreation.

"Community service is a factor in the league standings. So it's not just about sport, it's about being out in the community doing positive things," said Mann. "In the second year, we devised a means of using community service projects completed by the team as the tie-breaker in league standings."

And it worked.

"We saw in the first year pretty much every team did multiple community service things that led to at least a couple thousand hours of volunteer time in 10 weeks across the city."

There was also plenty of bonding and fun. After each game, the league would host a bar night at a different neighborhood establishment, regularly drawing over 400 people.

One of them was Detroit native Tania Bennett Allen, a paralegal who lives in Indian Village, a historic district on the city's east side that was listed on the National Register of Historic Places in 1972.[2] Like most, Allen was first drawn to the league as a recreational activity.

"I have been involved with the DCFL since its first year. So I watched the league go from 11 teams to 30 teams. I joined the league because I remember when I played soccer in high school and how much fun I had, and it's an excellent way to stay fit," said Allen. "I have always been someone who enjoyed the outdoor sports so this was a perfect fit. Having the ability to run down people nearly half your age does build up your endurance."

"For a lot of us, those first couple of weeks of the season are brutal. We compare bruises and sprains, but by the end of the season, we are left wanting more. Weekday Warriors, I say. And I wouldn't spend a Tuesday evening any other way."

As an Indian Village resident, Allen was already part of a strong neighborhood identity that had proudly held its own through the city's most turbulent years. The Historic Indian Village Association was formed in 1937, dedicated to protecting its legacy as a prestigious residential district. Through the decades, the Association has staunchly defended its single-family residential zoning, and building and use restrictions.[3]

Within the boundaries of a few blocks on Burns, Iroquois, and Seminole Streets between Jefferson and Mack Avenues, architecture buffs can feast their eyes on over 350 stately examples of Colonial Revival, Tudor Revival, Renaissance Revival, Spanish Mission Revival, Federal, and Georgian Revival styles built in the early 20th century by prominent architects for some of Detroit's most illustrious residents, including Edsel Ford, son of Henry Ford, and automotive entrepreneur Henry Leland, founder of the Lincoln and Cadillac brands.[4]

Indian Village joined with adjacent West Village, a trendy historic district of upscale single and two-family houses, apartment buildings, and commercial structures spread over 20 square blocks, to form The Villages team.

But within the new city soccer league, Allen found an even more powerful sense of identity and community.

"Within that first year, I developed friendships with not only people in my neighborhood, but with people throughout the city," said Allen. "Now imagine doing this with approximately 1,000 men and women from diverse social, professional, and ethnic backgrounds. The league reminds me of the UN.

"I find myself out and people say my name and give me a high-five. If I don't know them I say to myself with a smile, it must be from soccer."

In year two, the league grew to 600 participants and 22 neighborhoods. There was so much interest across the entire metropolitan region that the organizers realized they needed to do something to keep the league focused on local community rather than the sport. Rules were established that each team captain has to actually live in the neighborhood he or she represents, and no team can have more than five members who aren't city residents.

"There has to be a genuine effort to recruit within the neighborhood. It wasn't to be exclusionary of the suburbs, it was about being an organizing tool within the neighborhood, said Mann."

By this time, the post-game celebrations had become so popular, that the host bars were running out of beer by the second hour. At this point, the league began hosting pop-up beer gardens around town in underutilized spaces such as parks and warehouses.

"These kinds of social settings have created amazing connections," said Mann. "You'll see Jamaican immigrants hanging out with suburbanites who just moved into the city and are looking to explore. The age range is from a couple players in their early 60s, and most in their late 20s and 30s, to a couple 18-year-olds."

They also launched a tournament at season's end,

the Copa Detroit, which culminates in a huge picnic next to the playing fields on historic Belle Isle. To promote it, they teamed up with local graphic designers to develop iconic posters for the annual Copa, which have become instant collectors' items. Each year's all-day tournament is attended by more than 1,000 people, with teams bringing their tents, grills, and food to share. The first Copa Detroit was won by The Villages, Allen's own Detroit Riverfront community.

"Most teams don't mind losing in the first round because they end up hanging around drinking beer and having a good time," joked Mann.

In fact, the league and its season-ending gathering have become such a potent expression of community, Allen decided to take it upon herself to find ways to keep the soccer players bonded throughout the year.

"At last year's Copa, I was just looking around the field of 30 teams and said to myself, why does this have to end? We are all having a great time, enjoying each other's company. Let's keep it going," said Allen. "So I started reaching out to various professional teams in Detroit—Wings, Tigers, Lions, Pistons—and said 'hey, this is who we are and as a team we'd like to come out and show support to our hometown professional teams.' We weren't looking for free tickets, just a block so that we can come out and sit together as a team."

"Well, everyone loved it! We've gone to see the Wings and got to take photos on the ice afterwards. The Lions gave us a block of free tickets, which was very generous of them. And the Pistons brought us out on party buses and limos and fed us at an awesome price."

By year three, there were 28 neighborhoods and 800 participants, using virtually every available field in the city. Teams began adopting youth teams to coach. Older captains would move on to become referees and umpires.

A BEAUTIFUL FUTURE

While "the beautiful game" has undeniably taken a place in its own right in Detroit's ongoing legacy as a sports town, the DCFL website also gives a nod of respect (and a direct link) to a far older Detroit tradition of community athletics: Detroit PAL (Detroit Police Athletic League), a major youth athletics nonprofit initiative that serves over 10,000 Detroit kids. Founded in 1969 by the Detroit Police Department's Youth Bureau in the shadow of the 1967 Detroit riots, Detroit PAL struggled through decades of financial and political strife, finally merging with Think Detroit in 2006 to form Think Detroit PAL.[5] The organization is now working to build a new headquarters on the site of the old Tiger Stadium.[6]

In 2012, the Detroit City FC was formed as a minor league soccer team that plays in the National Premier Soccer League's (NPSL) Midwest Great Lakes Conference. Built on the same spirit of Detroit civic pride and partnerships that promote small community businesses, Detroit City FC has established itself as one of the most talked-about soccer teams in North America, and the grassroots embodiment of a resurgent city.[7] The team regularly draws crowds of 2,000–3,000 fans. Local musicians have created songs to celebrate the team. A local brewery has crafted a signature Detroit City FC brew.

The current stable of team sponsors is as diverse

as the city itself: Core Power protein drinks; Slows To Go BBQ; Green Dot Stables, a restaurant and bar on West Lafayette; Detroit Bikes, a hip local bicycle manufacturer; Wheelhouse Detroit, a bike rental company; and El Guapo Fresh Mexican Grill.

The talented roster has included players from major Michigan colleges including the University of Michigan, Michigan State University, Western Michigan University, Saginaw Valley State University, and Oakland University, as well as Bowling Green State University in Ohio, Syracuse University in New York, Butler University in Indiana, Georgetown University in Washington, D.C., and the University of New Hampshire. Some have gone on to the professional ranks, replaced by equally talented newcomers as the team's reputation grows.

Detroit City FC—affectionately nicknamed Le Rouge—emerged from the 12-game 2013 Great Lakes Division season with a record of 11 wins, 1 tie, and 0 losses. Detroit City FC was the Great Lakes regular season champions, the Rust Belt Derby trophy winners, and finished the regular season as the #1 ranked team in the 57-team NPSL.[8]

Media attention included a March 2012 interview with team co-owners Alex Wright and Ben Steffans on WJR's Destination 313 Program with local radio celebrities Paul W. Smith and Stephen Luigi Piazza. In the interview, Wright and Steffans talked about the rising popularity of soccer and what it means to be an owner of a sports team in Detroit.[9]

But in a city beset with bankruptcy and massive infrastructure problems, Mann admits there's a limit to how much neighborhood soccer can achieve as a conduit between civic energy and city government.

Meanwhile, the neighborhood league that inspired it all continues to thrive in its own right, staying true to its original mission.

At least six teams have adopted a vacant lot or unused park within their neighborhood and converted it into a soccer field, keeping it mowed and adding goals.

"It's one of the tangential things you didn't anticipate happening when you started, but it's turned from bringing people together and making connections, into people actually adopting spaces," said Mann. "All kinds of unique and different partnerships have developed that you never could have anticipated."

For example, in Mann's own Hubbard Farms neighborhood, the soccer team's communications network has morphed into a highly effective text messaging emergency alert system that utilizes "flash mob" technology to respond in real time to crime and other emergencies.

"A lot of times when crimes are happening, the police response is very slow, so we'll send out a text message through the system created in the soccer team, and you'll see half a dozen soccer team members and neighbors respond."

The alerts have even saved Mann's own home from break-ins several times.

"It's all because of a very simple, effective way to bring people together."

The league now has an annual operating budget of about $17,000, which is mainly generated from individual player dues of $20 per season. The funds are mainly used for field rentals, referees, and equipment such as new goals. The league operates as an LLC with five owners, one of whom operates as the league commissioner. The organization is heavily structured around the captains of the neighborhood teams who are chosen by their teammates. With considerable input from the captains at annual meetings, the owners of the league make all of the final decisions.[10]

After four seasons, the league has 32 teams representing nearly as many Detroit neighborhoods, with close to 1,000 people participating. Mann said that over 50 people have cited the DCFL as their reason for moving into the city of Detroit.

"Everyone out there believes in the city. By playing with a small ball, we have already managed to make a positive change in the city of Detroit," said Allen. "If anyone was new to the city or just wanted to increase your circle of friends, I would say, come to a game or join a team. You'll find yourself invited to dinner or brunch by 15 different people by the end of the day."

Their presence even appears to be having a positive, if indirect impact, on city services.

"A lot of members of the league are young professionals new to the city, with a natural cynicism toward the local government in Detroit. But the league has shown, by activating a space, you put pressure on the city to step up," said Mann. "It's like the soccer fields at Belle Isle are mowed more than other places because we have 1,000 people out there utilizing them. In other places where the parks are being used, it's changing the (maintenance) schedule. Connections are being made with city staff handling maintenance who see how parks are being used. It's not formal, but as the city grapples with fewer resources, it's one way to show the city where facilities are being used so those resources can be used more effectively."

Still, there's no denying the transformative power of a simple soccer game.

In its second year, the Copa Detroit was won by the team from Brightmoor, a formerly thriving working-class neighborhood that has come to symbolize urban decay for much of the media and many people outside Detroit. Over the decades of the city's worst decline, its four square miles had eroded into a landscape of abandoned homes and weed-choked vacant lots that became a convenient dumping ground for garbage and a favorite haunt for drug dealers and prostitutes. In 2011, the Detroit Free Press reported that Brightmoor's median household income was $17,346. More than a third of its homes were vacant, and most of the residents who remained simply couldn't afford to leave. In a single stretch of about 18 city blocks in Brightmoor, 15 people had been found murdered from February 2004 to July 2010.[11]

In the past several years, that's all begun to change as nonprofit organizations, community alliances, and the private sector have taken an active interest in the neighborhood's plight, while a city initiative to demolish vacant buildings has been a crucial step in cleaning up criminal hotspots. Neighbors Building Brightmoor and the Brightmoor Alliance are among the grassroots efforts working to mobilize the community for positive growth and change. In January of 2014, the Detroit Blight Authority announced plans to demolish at least another 117 blighted buildings in a 35-block section of Brightmoor, continuing the positive momentum.[12]

In 2012, The Villages took back the Copa Detroit crown from rival Brightmoor. But the most anticipated match of the tournament that year was the Brightmoor Dragons versus Berry Subdivision, a historic district reported to be the neighborhood with the most expensive homes in Detroit, with a median worth of $300,000 according to the 2000 Census.[13]

But none of the local sports reporters covering the Copa Detroit 2012 were talking about the two neighborhoods' demographic extremes.

As far as Detroit's avid soccer fans were concerned, Brightmoor and Berry simply had the league's top talent.[14]

And that pretty much says it all.

(ENDNOTES)

1 "Welcome to Hubbardfarms.org," Hubbard Farms, accessed April 1, 2014, http://hubbardfarms.org.

2 "National Register Information System." National Register of Historic Places. National Park Service. 2007-01-23.

3 "The Historic Indian Village Association," Historic Indian Village Association & Indian Village Men's & Women's Garden Clubs, accessed April 7, 2014, http://www.historicindianvillage.org/about/.

4 "Indian Village, Detroit," Wikipedia, accessed April 7, 2014, http://www.en.wikipedia.org/wiki/Indian_Village_Detroit.

5 "Detroit PAL History," Detroit Police Athletic League, copyright 2013, accessed April 7, 2014, http://www.detroitpal.org/about/PAL_history.asp.

6 "Detroit PAL Will Bring Baseball Back to the Corner of Michigan and Trumbull in 2015," Detroit Police Athletic League, accessed April 7, 2014, http://thinkdetroit.org/index.asp.

7 "About Us," Detroit City Football Club, accessed April 2, 2014, http://www.detcityfc.com/.

8 "Looking Ahead," Detroit City Football Club, accessed April 7, 2014, http://www.detcityfc.com/news.

9 "In the Media: Detroit City FC Interview by WJR's Paul W. Smith," Detroit City Football Club, accessed April 7, 2014, http://www.detcityfc.com/news/in-the-media/.

10 "The Detroit City Futbol League," Michigan Municipal League, accessed April 2, 2014, http://placemaking.mml.org/detroit-city-futbol-league/.

11 Suzette Hackney and Kristi Taylor, "How Brightmoor Became a Hotspot for Homicides," Detroit Free Press, November 14, 2011, accessed April 2, 2014, http://www.freep.com/article/20111114/NEWS01/311140001/How-Brightmoor-became-hot-spot-homicides.

12 Kirk Pinho, "Blight Authority Targets Additional 21-Block Area of Brightmoor," Crain's Detroit Business, January 20, 2014, revised January 21, 2014, accessed April 2, 2014, http://www.crainsdetroit.com/article/20140120/news/140129996/blight-authority-targets-additional-21-block-area-of-brightmoor#.

13 "Berry Subdivision Historic District," Encyclopedia of Detroit, Detroit Historical Society, accessed April 2, 2014, http://detroithistorical.org/learn/encyclopedia-of-detroit/berry-subdivision-historic-district.

14 Fletcher Sharpe, "Detroit Copa Soccer Tournament Wraps Up with The Villages Taking the Title," Mlive.com, August 6, 2011, accessed April 2, 2014, http://www.mlive.com/soccer/index.ssf/2012/08/copa_iii_wraps_up_in_detroit_as_the_villages_takes_title.html.

CASE STUDY

Detroit Soup

Detroit, Michigan — Pop. 713,777

PROJECT SCOPE

Back in 2010, a group of social entrepreneurs wanted to improve their Detroit community in various unique ways, but needed their neighbors' support to do it. Inspired by InCUBATE, an innovative neighborhood arts funding program in Chicago, they organized the first Detroit SOUP in February 2010 as a crowdfunding potluck that brings people together to raise money and support for community projects. Attendees make a suggested donation of $5 and listen to pitches from people doing great things in their community—anything from cleaning up a park, to running an after-school program, to starting a small business. Over a potluck-style dinner, attendees connect, ask questions, share ideas, and then vote on the project they like the best. The winner leaves with all of the money raised at the door to carry out their project, and then attends a future SOUP to report on their progress. Past winners include a wide range of projects, and the only criteria for submitting a proposal is that the project has to benefit the city.

Detroit SOUP's vision is to work with key community leaders to help change the way people engage with the democratic process by establishing neighborhood relational hubs across the city. Detroit SOUP's monthly Citywide SOUPs draw a crowd of anywhere from 100 to 300 people. Attendees toss their $5 into a soup pot as they walk through the front door. The size of the donation is based solely on the number of participants who attend and donate to the pot. At Citywide SOUPs, the winner usually goes home with $700–$2,000.

Detroit SOUP also helps support neighborhood-specific dinners in communities across Detroit, Hamtramck, and Highland Park, two inner-ring suburbs. These dinners occur quarterly and usually attract a smaller audience and fewer donations. Most neighborhood dinners are able to raise anywhere from $200–$1,000 for neighborhood-specific projects.

INVESTMENT

>> The cost for running a SOUP can and should be minimal and is therefore more sustainable. Organizers are usually volunteers and the venue, food, and other materials are usually donated. The hardest costs to get around are printing flyers and materials for the actual event (bowls, sporks, cups, voting box, resource board, tables, and chairs, etc.).

>> SOUP organizing groups usually start with no capital, but some local grants and key community partnerships can help with funding startup and sustainability. Some SOUP organizing groups do small-scale fundraising at the actual event by promoting SOUP, asking for donations for drinks, etc. to support expenses. It's best to reserve all of the money raised at the door for the winning project. It can be helpful for SOUP organizing groups to partner with community nonprofits, businesses, or institutions to print flyers, offer storage space for materials, and help with low-cost outreach initiatives.

SOCIOECONOMIC IMPACT

>> From the first dinner in February of 2010 to the April 2014 Citywide SOUP, a total of 71 Detroit SOUP dinners have raised nearly $67,000 for Detroit-specific projects. In 2013, more than 4,000 people gathered at Detroit SOUP dinners across the city where they shared countless connections, resources, and ideas.

>> In 2013, Detroit SOUP began helping interested neighborhoods start their own neighborhood-specific dinners. As of April 2014, there were nine resident groups in Detroit, Hamtramck, and Highland Park who plan, facilitate, and execute their own quarterly SOUP dinners to raise money for localized projects.

>> During this time period, SOUP winners have included 10 small businesses, 15 community cleanups or beautification projects, 6 food or urban agriculture related projects, 5 art projects, and at least 15 projects related to youth development. Some winners were one-time events, but many have continued through the months and years since they won support at SOUP.

>> Detroit SOUP attendance is often targeted at the neighborhood or community in which the dinner is held, but anyone is welcome to come. Citywide SOUP events often attract a large audience of Detroiters, suburban residents, out-of-town visitors, and people with interests in placemaking, social justice, and Detroit.

LESSONS LEARNED

>> Create a small board of key stakeholders – To coordinate SOUP dinners, it's important to engage people from across the community: residents, nonprofits, churches, businesses, neighborhood associations, etc. This group of 5–10 participants will be able to plan, do outreach, and facilitate SOUP dinners.

>> Finding the right people to start a SOUP dinner is key– SOUP boards should be diverse and representative of the community in order to establish the best goals for the event, expand partnerships, and draw the largest audience possible. Try to find the people who might not always volunteer for things—the younger, more creative residents and members of different cultural groups are often a good place to start.

>> Outline group vision, goals and values – Before the board begins planning, it's important for everyone to share the same vision, goals, and values for the dinner. Why are you doing this in the first place? What do you hope to accomplish? Outlining these early on help smooth decision-making and make it easier to track progress.

>> Divide board roles and responsibilities – Everyone on the SOUP board should have an important and active role. At the minimum, the SOUP team should have a lead coordinator, secretary, treasurer, outreach chair, potluck food chair, and a proposal chair to manage project submissions. Everyone should feel valued and involved, without being overworked.

>> Create a timeline – Make sure everyone is on the same page. The board will need to find a great location for the event, set the event date, a proposal submission deadline, and start outreach.

>> Do outreach – The most important aspect to the dinner is people. Each board member should encourage their friends, family, neighbors, business partners, and everyone in the community to attend the event. Print flyers, create an online presence, make presentations at community events—do everything to spread the word on how to submit a proposal and to get people to attend the dinner.

>> Plan event logistics – Boards will need to select presenters for the event, finalize logistics for the venue, and make sure there are enough food donations and materials. Board members will need to build an agenda and divide roles for each person during the actual event.

>> Host the SOUP dinner – Have fun, talk to your neighbors, meet someone new, and encourage others to do the same. Take pictures at the event and document details of the dinner (number of attendees, money raised, winning project details, etc.). Celebrate the success of your SOUP!

>> Debrief and grow – After each dinner, it's important for the board to gather feedback from SOUP attendees and to meet as a group to debrief the event. From the discussion, create a to-do list to continue things that are going well and improve on issues the group outlined.

>> Sustain – To be successful, SOUPs should occur regularly (monthly, bi-monthly, or quarterly). The board should work to establish a SOUP model that works best in their own community.

>> Be a role model - Detroit SOUP's success has inspired similar grassroots fundraising efforts elsewhere in Michigan, such as Jonesville SOUP, which raised funds for community projects proposed by Jonesville High School students in 2013.

>> Start with the right people – Getting a great board together is the best way to host a successful dinner. SOUP can't happen with one organizer, it needs to be a collaborative effort of community residents, businesses, and local institutions. Create an environment that is creative, collaborative, and can focus on the goals of the dinner.

>> Limit rules – Detroit SOUP only has two rules: (1) Projects have to benefit Detroit or the specific neighborhood hosting the dinner and (2) Presenters can't use technology in their presentation (it keeps the playing field equal, reduces issues related to technology, and keeps the short presentations engaging). SOUP is a fun, creative project, so boards should avoid too many rules— allow for creativity!

>> Avoid complication – Becoming a nonprofit is a lot of work and there's no real reason to become one to carry out SOUP events. If funding is available and necessary, it can be helpful to partner with a neighborhood nonprofit in order to act as a fiduciary for small grants, use their meeting space, and store SOUP supplies. Avoid the time and legal issues of becoming a formal 501c3, unless the community and board really push for it.

>> Keep it going – SOUP spreads from word-of-mouth. The longer you can sustain SOUP dinners the better! More people will come, connect, raise money, and do great things in the community.

>> A SOUP "How-To" guide and other information is available at www.detroitsoup.com.

Moving Placemaking Forward Through

Civic Engagement

• Effective civic engagement is a key strategy for successful placemaking. It is important communities recognize that placemaking is both about the physical place AND the making of it. With strong engagement, governments can improve decision-making and residents are more informed, invested, and have greater support for local initiatives. Learn more about Civic engagement in placemaking from the Michigan Municipal League.[1]

• What is Civic Engagement? We've all heard that attracting and keeping talent is the creative lifeblood of any city seeking to grow into the 21st century and beyond. But placemaking can't work without people— and that means connecting people quickly to the other bright people, places, and work they're passionate about. Check out this video from the Michigan Municipal League's 2010 Annual Convention.[2]

• Civic engagement should be at the forefront of placemaking projects. Start a conversation on engagement and citizen participation in your community. Here are some talking points from the Michigan Municipal League to share with neighbors, organizations, and especially local government officials.[3]

• *Places in the Making: How Placemaking Builds Places and Communities,* MIT Department of Urban Studies and Planning. A deep look into placemaking: challenges, case studies, lessons, and evaluation techniques with a primary focus on the importance of process over product in placemaking activities.[4]

• *Assessing Public Engagement Effectiveness: Rapid Review Worksheets,* Institute for Local Government.

Local officials are increasingly using a range of public engagement strategies. However, officials spend little time assessing how these processes worked for the local agency and community. This document offers Rapid Review Worksheets to evaluate strategies and implement more effective engagement.[5]

• *Public Deliberation: A Manager's Guide to Citizen Engagement;* The Business of Government, 2006.

The purpose of this citizen engagement guide is to strengthen the foundation for participatory governance within the federal government, particularly in agency decision-making. The guide provides examples of experimentation with new engagement techniques, thereby encouraging federal managers to see themselves as potential agents within the movement to reinvigorate democratic governance.[6]

• *Stronger Citizens, Stronger Cities: Changing Governance Through a Focus on Place;* Project for Public Spaces, March 17, 2013.

Functioning cities and creating a great place requires more than urban planners. This article highlights the importance of resident participation in all aspects of the democratic process.[7]

• *Creating a Culture of Learning: A Framework for Neighborhood Public Work; Neighborhood Learning Community,* Minnesota's Center for Democracy and Citizenship, 2008.

This framework is intended for adults who are working to create a neighborhood that works for kids and uses a unique theory of change. The document outlines guiding principles, organizing tools, and action worksheets to help communities establish their own unique framework for creating better public spaces.[8]

• *Connected Communities: Local Governments as a Partner in Citizen Engagement and Community Building,* Edited by James Svara and Sarah Denhardt.

This White Paper outlines steps to take in developing partnerships with citizens and community organizations that strengthen engagement and foster community. It explores the methods to form a comprehensive and integrated approach to citizen engagement that creates the connected community.[9]

(ENDNOTES)

1 Sarah Craft, "Civic Engagment in Placemaking," Michigan Municipal League, May 29, 2014, http://placemaking.mml.org/2014/05/29/civic-engagement-in-placemaking/.

2 Josh McManus, "Civic Engagement: The Act of Being the Change You Want to be in the World," 2011, http://placemaking.mml.org/videos/?catid=category&slg=what-is-civic-engagement.

3 "Engagement," Michigan Municipal League, accessed June 10, 2014, http://placemaking.mml.org/engagement/.

4 "Places in the Making: How Placemaking Builds Places and Communities," Department of Urban Studies and Planning (DUSP) at Massachusetts Institute of Technology (MIT), 2013, http://dusp/mit.edu/sites/all/files/attachments/project/mit-dusp-places-in-the-making.

5 "Assessing Public Engagement Effectiveness: Rapid Review Worksheets," Institute for Local Government, accessed June 10, 2014, http://www.ca-ilg.org/post/assessing-public-engagement-effectiveness-rapid-review-worksheets.

6 Carolyn J. Lukensmeyer and Lars Hasselblad Torres, "Public Deliberation: A Manager's Guide to Civic Engagement," 2006, http://www.businessofgovernment.org/report/public-deliberation-managers-guide-citizen-engagement.

7 "Stronger Citizens, Stronger Cities: Changing Governance Through a Focus on Place," Project for Public Spaces, March 20, 2013, http://www.resilience.org/stories/2013-03-20/stronger-citizens-stronger-cities-changing-governance-through-a-focus-on-place.

8 Kari Dennissen, Nan Skelton and Nan Kari, "Creating a Culture of Learning: A Framework for Neighborhood Public Work," Minnesota's Center for Democracy and Citizenship, West Side Neighborhood Learning Community, 2008, http://web.augsburg.edu/cdc/NLCFinalVersion.pdf.

9 James Svara and Sarah Denhardt, ed.,"Connected Communities: Local Governments as a Partner in Citizen Engagement and Community Building," October 15, 2010, http://icma.org/en/icma/knowledge_network/documents/kn/document/301763.

Looking for a way to inject new energy into your local economy? Start hunting for gazelles. Or better yet, start cultivating the gazelles you might already have in your own backyard.

Back in 1994, economist David Birch coined the term "gazelles" to describe rapid-growth small businesses: enterprises whose sales doubled every four years. These "gazelles" represent only 4 percent of all U.S. companies, but are responsible for 70 percent of all new jobs, compared to the "elephants" (like Wal-Mart) and "mice" (corner barbershops).[1]

And it goes way beyond job creation and making money. These are the innovative entrepreneurs who light a fire across the landscape with their high-energy visions that can transform a community and revitalize and reinvent its sense of place.

Here's what Charlie Gandy at Project for Public Spaces, a nonprofit dedicated to creating dynamic public spaces, says about it: "What happens when local small businesses bring a healthy dose of creative talent and out-of-the-box thinking to their entrepreneurial mix? What happens when they see themselves as progressive artisans and thought leaders and feel empowered to spread their enthusiasm with fellow local business owners? Business zones in cities and towns that were once depressed and/or even blighted are resurrected and revived. Economic prosperity blooms and grows in fresh and remarkable ways."[2]

Not every business is a gazelle, of course. They're usually fairly young companies—25 years or less—and they could pop up in any kind of industry, from technology to food service. Also, it can be nearly impossible to tell at a company's launch whether it will succeed or fail. Gazelles are rare. Even more rare are the gazelles described by Gandy: those who go beyond their own success to lift up the entire community around them.

But sometimes all it takes is one. So take a good, hard look around. If you spot one, feed it and help it grow. Then sit back and watch what happens.

(ENDNOTES)

1 Joshua Zumbrun, "Hunting for Gazelles," Forbes, October 30, 2009, http://www.forbes.com/forbes/2009/1116/careers-small-businesses-unemployment-hunting-for-gazelles.html.

2 Charlie Gandy, "Gazelles and the Art of Placemaking," Project for Public Spaces, June 25, 2012, https://www.pps.org/blog/gazelles-the-art-of-placemaking/.

ENTREPRENEURSHIP

Feeding a Community's Heart and Soul

As the first shock waves of global and knowledge-based economies began to emerge, Michigan's successful automotive narrative of the 20th century began to unravel. We built cars to feed the American dream—but then it slowly became the national nightmare in the 21st century. Roads couldn't be built wide and fast enough to accommodate cars and sprawling development. We were driving so fast, we didn't notice the disintegration of our communities, or if we did, we didn't think about its consequences. As changing demographics began to reshape our future, old ways of meeting these challenges became outdated.

Freshly-minted college graduates began fleeing Michigan to find an urban experience that would provide transit options, walkability, a rich cultural experience, and housing options that they couldn't find in Michigan. Unthinkable in previous generations when people followed the jobs, they were now looking for a place first, then seeking work. We had to figure out a way to keep them here. The answer is investing in our own communities, and building the types of places with the amenities they seek. If finding a place first, then looking for a job, is the new order, creating an open entrepreneurial environment is critical to making Michigan a place that can attract and retain talent and compete on a global level.

LOCAL FIRST

A step inside Zingerman's Delicatessen stirs all the senses. Whether you are a first-time visitor or a repeat customer, it is a place that always delivers an experience that begs for more. Located in the heart of Ann Arbor's historic Kerrytown neighborhood, its distinctive whimsical art, the smells emanating from the open kitchen, the bustling noise of customers of all ages, and the enticing taste of a fresh deli sandwich in your hands never disappoint.

Although Zingerman's has been satisfying the palates of hundreds of thousands of customers for over 30 years with its fresh and flavorful food, signature coffee, and delectable baked goods, its focus on nourishing the heart and soul of the community uniquely defines this business. It has demonstrated the powerful impact local businesses can have in the community, and continually shows why it is so critical to support and invest locally.

This is a story of a delicatessen, but a story that goes beyond the pastrami and corned beef sandwiches on rye that would normally define a deli.

It all began in 1982, when two men, Paul Saginaw and Ari Weinzweig, envisioned opening up their own traditional deli in Ann Arbor, home of the University of Michigan, just like the ones they grew up with in Detroit and Chicago. But there is nothing traditional about the way they have run this iconic institution. This entrepreneurial duo laid out a business plan with a foundation of innovation and entrepreneurial activity that would not only lead to business success, but have a powerful socioeconomic impact on the community in which they lived.

Boasting over 600 employees today and over $50 million in annual sales, Zingerman's humble beginnings consisted of a small brick building with just two employees. With recent additions to accommodate the growing business, the original brick building now houses only the retail store with over 300 types of cheese, stacks of bread from the Bakehouse, and an impressive collection of delectable olive oils, sauces, and condiments. Rather than build on their success by opening hundreds of additional delis around the

country, the founders made the bold decision to nurture their roots within the community and cultivate growth opportunities for their own employees.

This focus on employee investment has led to nine additional unique businesses under the Zingerman's Community of Businesses umbrella. Each business was borne out of encouragement to innovate, passion to create, and support to succeed. Weinzweig states in his blog, "We chose to create what we call the Zingerman's Community of Businesses—a collection of Zingerman's businesses, each with its own food specialty, all located in the Ann Arbor area, each working to help make the shopping and eating in every aspect of Zingerman's more flavorful and more enjoyable than ever. In each business we've sought out a managing partner or partners so that there will be someone to bring the day-to-day passion and persistence that it takes to be really good at anything into play on a day-to-day basis. Paul and I are there to provide guidance, support, leadership, and whatever else we need to do, which includes

everything from writing this essay to lots of tasting, tracking down great food, contributing to the community, providing plenty of training classes, leadership work at all levels, all the way through clearing tables and emptying the trash."[1]

"Zingerman's is a business incubator," Saginaw said. "We acculturate you and then help you grow. It's like a junior college curriculum/long-term training program, and we provide administrative and technical expertise that start-up businesses need but can rarely afford. Ongoing businesses are subsidizing the start-up businesses. It is a different model. We have a shared brand, a mission, and a set of guiding principles and vision. A lot of what we do could be replicated. It's sustainable."

Not all of the businesses relate to food, however. In addition to baked goods, old-fashioned candy, and handcrafted cheese,

Zingerman's has parlayed its praiseworthy customer service, along with many of their management systems, into consulting and training seminars for businesses and organizations from around the world. In the spring of 2014, they opened their newest business, Cornman Farms events space. Although it is a meat, dairy, and vegetable farm that is sourced to Zingerman's Roadhouse restaurant, Cornman Farms consists of a historic farmhouse and barn on 27 acres of farmland. Plans call for connecting the buildings by a covered walkway, and using the site to host weddings, parties, dinners, and other private events.[2]

For one entrepreneur, however, it really is all about the food. Just out of high school, Charlie Frank can still remember his first Zingerman's Reuben in 1984. He says he never really aspired to work in a deli, but ended up doing a short stint at Zingerman's. Fast forward to more than 10 years later and a quick chance meeting with one of the founders who shared his vision for opening up more businesses, and Frank knew what he had to do. Although the flavor and experience of that Reuben sandwich has remained forever etched in his memory, it was visions of sugar plums—or something sweet, anyway—that danced in his head. He loved pastries and was fortunate to be quickly hired at the Bakehouse as manager of the pastry department. The managing partners were very supportive of why he was really there—to learn how to run a business and embark on his own someday.

Less than two years later, Frank decided that it was time to dip his fingers into the chocolate. "I decided to make candy bars and spend the rest of my life doing it," he says. So candy began to be made alongside the pastries.

It was sold as if it was a pastry—always fresh. In 2005, Zzang bars were introduced and quickly named "the ultimate handmade candy bar" by Chocolatier Magazine.[3]

With growing candy sales, he decided it was time to open his own business. In 2009, with the company's full support, he rented space at the Bakehouse and opened Zingerman's Candy Manufactory. Several years into this successful business, Frank's enthusiasm has not waned. He says that "an entrepreneur is about being passionate and bringing joy. There are not enough hours in the day. Every day is a thrill to make such delicious stuff. This is what a candy bar should taste like—or this is what fudge should taste like when just made. There are so many fun things to do with sugar that you want to share it with people. It is so refreshing to be a part of a business that supports entrepreneurs and believes in your passion."

THE RIPPLE EFFECT

Maker Works is another powerful example of how Zingerman's supports and encourages their employees to continually challenge themselves in creative and innovative ways. Tom Root, an affable man who clearly loves what he does, even on a Monday morning, "grew up" in the culture of Zingerman's. With a passion for business and entrepreneurship, his path to Zingerman's came via a trip to San Francisco with his wife, who was the buyer for the deli. They heard about a food mail order company as a stand-alone business, so upon their return, Root suggested to Zingerman's that they augment the already existing mail order business by creating a separate complimentary online business. Receptive to the idea, Zingermans.com was opened in 1999. After three years, it merged with the mail order

company. Through his work, Root pioneered the use of lean manufacturing[4] within Zingerman's, as well as led and introduced open book financial management within the company, and truly learned what service means–to be a good citizen and serve your community.

These ideals triggered another idea for Root. Fearing for the number of people who would find themselves unemployed during the Great Recession of 2008, particularly in the southeast region of Michigan, he again turned to an idea he had heard about on the west coast—commercial worker space that was run like a business. He felt that this could potentially be part of a solution to so many highly-skilled people losing their jobs, giving them the opportunity to turn themselves into self-sustaining independent contractors and opening their own businesses. But first, they would need access to high-cost capital equipment.

Two years ago, Root's dream finally came to fruition when he co-founded Maker Works, created out of service to the community, but in a commercial context–self-sustaining and run like a business.

Maker Works allows people to rent fabrication equipment to invent and build things. The cost is leveraged over a large membership. Equipment can be rented by the hour, day, week, month, or year. It's all about the networking opportunities that present themselves. It's about sharing ideas and not keeping a patent for oneself.

Root feels he has honored Zingerman's by showing that the same concepts and philosophies could work outside the Zingerman's brand. With a flexible work schedule, he continues to work mornings in the mail order business, and devotes the rest of the time to Maker Works. Saginaw threw his full support behind this concept. "Traditional business incubators don't work very well. Rather than expertise and content, they are just buying some cheap space. Success is measured by funding, not an idea being validated by the customers and turning opportunity into revenue."

Two success stories illustrate the synergy and creativity that have come from Maker Works. Following 22 years of designing exhibit space and furniture for the University of Michigan Natural History Museum, Alan McWaters wanted to grow SkyShips Designs, a company he had informally started 15 years ago, in which he designs and builds custom furniture meticulously crafted from renewable, exotic, and native hardwoods[5]. Maker Works was the perfect landing place for him, giving him access to tools and equipment to pursue his goals. He began to build his customer base at Maker Works from other entrepreneurs who needed custom furniture for the businesses they were trying to launch. McWaters has become a fixture at Maker Works, leasing space for his business and becoming part of the staff.

What does a start-up high-tech company have in common with a woodworker?

Sight Machine is a start-up high-tech company that uses Internet technologies to improve manufacturing. It manages a type of software called OpenCV, an open source software that does computer processing and video. A very large auto company needed a tunnel that would hold lights and cameras for their computer systems. So Sight Machine hired McWaters to build the tunnel, then they pitched their concept and landed a contract with the auto company. This is a company that started off with two guys and an 8x8 office. Now they occupy 3,500 square feet of office space in Maker Works. They recently landed $5 million in venture capital, and have hired several more employees. Shared space and mutual support have generated two success stories at opposite ends of the spectrum—one an artisanal woodworker interested in doing what he loves post-retirement, and the other a start-up high-tech company that is successfully on its way to playing in the big league.

LOCAL INVESTMENT, LOCAL COMMITMENT

When a local business is patronized and embraced by the community, the relationship becomes so much more than just a brief customer transaction—it becomes a familiar, comfortable place to go. It feeds the emotional connection to the community.

"Locally-owned and controlled businesses contribute to that sense of place," Saginaw explained ardently. "You are much more concerned about what goes on in the community because your kids go to the schools; homes are protected by the city; roads are taken care of; community wealth is redefined by block parties, safe streets, and clean water; so local businesses participate in the public sector to a much higher degree. Their owners and employees run for school boards, council seats, vote, and weigh in on public policy. However, with large manufacturers who come with the promise of job creation, communities often curry their favor with tax abatements and relaxed

zoning and environmental policies. These companies often will then desert that community as soon as it finds a way to produce or distribute its products more cheaply somewhere else after having bled the local treasuries dry, lowering the quality of life, and scorching the earth. Local businesses can have an enormous positive impact as a corporate citizen by taking significant action in the public sector that contributes to the social, cultural, and educational vitality of a community."

With an emphasis on alleviating hunger in their county, Zingerman's guiding principles state that it is their chosen responsibility to make substantial and significant contributions in order to strengthen the health, social, educational, and cultural fabric of this community.[6] Zingerman's has always had a strong connection to the local nonprofits. It's all about putting people and the community first. "Zingerman's wants to provide good lives for people and to be relevant," Saginaw said. "You don't have to wait to be successful to be generous. Generosity leads to success. If you can get your head around the idea that there exists such a thing as 'having enough', there is nothing more liberating than that. When you understand that, it allows you to experiment, to be extraordinary, and have more fun." Ten percent of their annual net operating profits are earmarked for giving back to the community through their donation program.

In 1988, Zingerman's started Food Gatherers in the basement of the deli, reinforcing the need to address hunger in the community. It was not only the first Michigan food rescue program, but the first program of its kind to be founded by a for-profit business.[7] It collects nutritious food from shops, restaurants, and hotels and quickly delivers it to people in need throughout the community. Today, Food Gatherers is an independent 501c3 not-for-profit organization governed by a board of directors, operated by 24 staff people, and more than 5,000 volunteers. It operates in partnership with more than 150 nonprofit agencies providing direct food assistance in the form of hot meals, nutritious snacks, or emergency groceries to low-income adults, seniors, and children throughout the county.[8]

Zingerman's generosity and outreach efforts extend internally as well. Five percent of annual net operating profits go to assist employees (or an immediate family member). This can come in the form of a loan, a grant, or through simply facilitating a connection in the community. Although many large companies have these types of programs, it's unusual to find them at smaller companies like Zingerman's.

EMPLOYEES MATTER

Zingerman's passion and creativity is reflected in the people they hire. It is a place where employees are encouraged to make changes, provide opinions, and participate in open and honest dialogues with one another. As part of every new employee orientation, a wide range of topics are covered. Customer service, diversity awareness, the meaning of a welcoming environment, and how to create a vision for their own financial success are all introduced to the new hire. Several committees have been formed internally to provide a level of discussion that can make real change.

Lynn Yates has been with the organization for almost 20 years now, following a circuitous route not unlike others who have started their working career at Zingerman's right out of college. She graduated from the University of Michigan, and although her goal was to go to medical school, a marriage intervened and she found herself working in the deli. When you ask her what makes her so passionate about working there, she enthusiastically shares one of her first memories—at 24 years old, she had written three pages of notes on ways to make work improvements in her area. She put them in co-founder Weinzweig's mail box and figured that was the end of it. But shortly after, he requested a meeting to discuss her ideas, several of which were instituted. This gave her enormous pride, making her feel part of something much greater. This was an organization that genuinely cared about employees' opinions. "When you're 24 years old, it's nice to know that you are involved in decisions and a real participant," Yates said.

Her skills and talent led to a variety of roles in the organization including sales, administrative services, marketing, and her current responsibilities of running the employee assistance program, called the Community Chest, and teaching courses on personal finance and diversity awareness as part of the new employee orientation. She said that she is working for a "company that is just not about profit—that's only one piece for them." Yates feels that she never gave up a dream in trading medical school for her work at Zingerman's. She's following her passion—helping people and making a difference in their lives—it's just in a deli, not a hospital.

With equal versatility and commitment, 29-year-old Robby Griswold is passionate about working at Zingerman's, because, he said, "so many basic cultural attitudes are upheld and actionable, and this is a business to help make the world better, stay profitable, but give back as much as possible." He also began his Zingerman's career following graduation with a liberal arts degree from the University of Michigan. Unlike his close friends who moved to Chicago after school, he decided to stay in Ann Arbor, work at Zingerman's, and figure out his next step. This led to his first post-college

job working in Zingerman's mail order business, followed by a move to the finance area.

Like Yates, as Griswold gained more experience and skills in the organization, it led to more leadership roles. As co-chair of the Diversity Committee, his goal is seeing Zingerman's operationalize their best intentions with inclusion. Zingerman's and its role in the community have inspired him to do business in a different way. "This organization was oriented to employ human beings, not robots. The company holds itself to a really high standard of service. It keeps all finances transparent and operationalizes these values." For now, at least, he has no plans to follow his friends to Chicago.

2020 VISION

Zingerman's commitment to growth and employee investment never wavers. Plans call for an increase of 15–18 related businesses; zero net waste and carbon footprint; the attainment of a racial profile of partnerships that will, at the very least, represent the racial profile of the county; a new educational program for a new business model, and more employee ownership where employees help control the decisions of Zingerman's, just as partners do. These aspirations would take anyone's breath away, but if you believe that old adage that the best predictor for future behavior is past behavior, then one can be certain that these goals will be realized.

With Zingerman's national profile, thanks to its mouth-watering food and loyal fan base, it has now become part of the national conversation to raise the minimum wage. Another goal is to see that they provide not just a livable wage, but a thrivable wage for all of their employees that will reflect the financial success of the organization. Saginaw joined other small business owners in Washington, D.C. to discuss the merits of raising minimum wages with the U.S. Department of Labor. Zingerman's has built their business around "enhancing the lives of as many people as [they] possibly can. Moving to a 'thrivable wage' is part of Zingerman's deeper commitment to their workers and an understanding that, as an employer, they're part of a larger ecosystem of workers, their families, and their communities, not just partners and shareholders."[9] Already, all part-time and full-time employees receive health and dental benefits and paid time off. After one year of employment, employees are eligible for a 401(k).

Saginaw's higher wage advocacy recently garnered more national attention when President Obama paid a visit to the deli. While enjoying a Reuben sandwich, the president said that "…one of the reasons I went was because the sandwiches are outstanding. The second reason, though, is Zingerman's is a business that treats its workers well, and rewards honest work with honest wages."[10]

KEEPING IT LOCAL

To compete globally, we have to invest locally. It's that simple. Michigan's economic turnaround is happening, and will continue to do so, because of businesses like Zingerman's and their investment in the community.

As Christopher Leinberger, one of the leading urban thinkers, said, "Expecting early 19th century or even mid-20th century governance structures to handle the challenges of the early 21st century is not realistic."[11] If Michigan hopes to facilitate economic growth and allow for the development of places to provide key services and amenities that contribute to a high quality of life, then good public policy needs to be in place.

When asked how policy can help local businesses, Saginaw said, "Most policy is set up to stop people from doing things. We can either play police and catch people when they are doing something wrong, or help people do something right." He went on to say, "If you are going to give tax abatements, then make them available to the local businesses as well. Level the playing field. Consider local businesses first."

Seeing themselves as part of a whole, not just profit makers, makes Zingerman's an inspirational leader in their community and beyond.

(ENDNOTES)

1 Ari Weinzweig, "What is Zingerman's Anyway?, Zingerman's Community of Businesses, accessed April 14, 2014, http://www.Zingermanscommunity.com/about-us/.

2 Lizzy Alfs, "Zingerman's Opens New Event Space on Farm Near Dexter," Mlive.com, May 15, 2014, accessed June 11, 2014, http://www.mlive.com/business/ann-arbor/index.ssf/2014/05/zingermans_new_events_space_no.html.

3 http://www.zingermans.com

4 "Lean Manufacturing," Wikipedia, accessed April 28, 2014, http://en.wikipedia.org/wiki/Lean_manufacturing.

5 "Sky Ships Design," Sky Ships Design, accessed April 24, 2014, http://www.skyshipdesign.com.

6 "Community Giving," Zingerman's Community of Businesses, accessed April 24, 2014, http://zingermanscommunity.com/about-us/community-giving.

7 "About Us," Food Gatherers, accessed June 12, 2014, http://foodgatherers.org/?module=Page&sID=about-us.

8 Ibid.

9 Sheila Bapat, "A New Direction for Restaurant Workers? Zingerman's and the 'Thriveable Wage'," RH Reality Check, March 4, 2013, http://rhrealitycheck.org/article/2013/03/04/a-new-direction-for-restaurant-workers-zingermans-and-the-thriveable-wage/.

10 Jessica Webster, "Waiting for President Obama at Zingerman's Deli," Mlive.com, April 3, 2014, http://www.mlive.com/news/ann-arbor/index.ssf/2014/04/waiting_for_the_president_obam.html.

11 Christopher Leinberger, "Place Management: Society's Missing Level of Governance", Economics of Place: The Value of Building Communities Around People, Michigan Municipal League, 2011.

CASE STUDY

Mark's Carts

Ann Arbor, Michigan — Pop. 113,934

PROJECT SCOPE

Capitalizing on a growing national trend of food carts/trucks, Mark's Carts brings people of all ages together by offering delicious local food and communal seating, which has generated energy and activity on the nearby streets and neighborhood. Each of the eight food carts is individually owned by the vendors, and each presents a different style of ethnic or regional food.

Mark Hodesh, owner of the Downtown Home and Garden store, was looking for ways to utilize his privately owned empty lot behind his already successful business. Although he was not thinking about a foodie movement as such, he was inspired by a pizza oven on wheels that he saw in Brooklyn, New York. He said it took him "five seconds" to come up with food carts, and thus, Mark's Carts was born.

INVESTMENT

>> Mark built a kitchen on his property, which is a legal requirement in order to serve food, and the linchpin of his idea. (It is also getting some off-season use from neighborhood restaurants that need the extra space.) Kitchen requirements vary from county to county, so it is important to check with the health department on equipment and design elements. Mark recommends sharing the menus with the county health department as well.

>> Each cart sits on a 40x75 foot lot.

>> The cost of a food cart can range from $6,000 to $20,000.

>> Fee for the season is $9,500 which includes:
- Access to the shared commissary kitchen
- Kitchen manager
- Daily cleaning
- Cleaning supplies
- Utilities

SOCIOECONOMIC IMPACT

>> Created 35 full-time and part-time jobs.

>> Two cart businesses have moved on to open permanent restaurants.

>> Sparked additional entrepreneurship on the same property with a seasonal beer garden adjacent to the food carts. This, in turn, has significantly increased the food cart evening business.

>> As an entry-level business to the food industry, food carts have offered people from all different socioeconomic backgrounds, the opportunity to potentially start a small, affordable business.

>> In addition to good food, creating a physical space allows people to sit and interact with those they don't know. Picnic tables provide excellent seating to encourage spontaneous conversations. Mark's Cart's has created a social "room" that encourages neighborhood social activity.

>> It's not just about the food. It's about creating a new social space and animating a previously dead space and street. Mark's Carts has helped transform the west edge of downtown. The owner remains flexible and open to other activities in the food courtyard, which has led to the wonderful additions of music and food tasting contests.

>> Raised more awareness of healthy, locally grown food.

>> Has brought an increase of business and foot traffic to Mark's Downtown Home and Garden store.

>> Within two blocks, a homemade ice cream store opened, and a year-round local produce store set up shop in an abandoned gas station.

>> An apartment building behind Mark's Carts is now complete and occupied.

LESSONS LEARNED

>> Keep it simple. Avoid expensive infrastructure costs. No heat in the winter? Close down—business is light anyway during the winter months.

>> Keep it flexible. Mark allows the carts to stay open as long as they want if there is business. (Some of the carts stay open to serve the beer garden customers.)

>> Be honest with yourself about what will realistically work for your community, but don't be afraid to try.

>> Contact the appropriate governing bodies upfront to make sure that everyone is on the same page.

>> Get buy-in from surrounding neighbors and businesses. Demonstrate how increased people traffic benefits everyone.

>> Use social media to market your business and engage the community.

For additional information:
Website: www.markscartsannarbor.com
Twitter: @MarksCartsA2
Facebook: www.Facebook.com/MarksCartsA2

Moving Placemaking Forward Through Entrepreneurship

• New Crowdfunding Law in Michigan – On December 20, 2013, Michigan enacted Public Act 264 and became one of the few states to authorize pioneering intrastate crowdfunding that will help lead the way for local investing. Known as "investment crowdfunding," this is a powerful economic development tool that allows people to take control of their community development by engaging directly in the process of supporting the businesses in which they believe. You can access everything you need to know at the Michigan Municipal League's crowdfunding website: www.crowdingmi.com.

• Small Business Association of Michigan – Helps Michigan small businesses succeed by promoting entrepreneurship, leveraging buying power, and engaging in political advocacy.[1]

• Accelerate Michigan Innovation Competition – This is an international business competition designed to highlight Michigan as a robust and vibrant venue for innovation and business opportunity. It showcases the best and brightest new business concepts to investment capital to help foster their growth within Michigan. It targets entrepreneurs with mid-to-late-seed-entrepreneurial businesses.[2]

• Resources for Entrepreneurs – This is a comprehensive directory of tools and resources for entrepreneurs, including specific information related to each of the individual states.[3]

• Michigan Economic Development Corporation (MEDC) – This is the state's marketing arm and lead advocate for business development, talent and jobs, tourism, film, digital media incentives, arts and cultural grants, and overall economic growth. The MEDC offers a number of business assistance services and capital programs for business attraction and acceleration, entrepreneurship, strategic partnerships, talent enhancement, and urban and community development.[4]

• Global Detroit Final Report – Global Detroit is an effort to revitalize southeast Michigan's economy by pursuing strategies that strengthen Detroit's connections to the world, and make the region more attractive and welcoming to immigrants, internationals, and foreign trade and investment as a means to produce jobs and regional economic growth.[5]

• Business Alliance For Local Living Economies (BALLE) – Their work is focused on creating real prosperity by connecting leaders, spreading solutions that work, and driving investment toward local economies.[6]

(ENDNOTES)

1 Small Business Association of Michigan, accessed June 12, 2014, https://www.sbam.org/.

2 "Accelerate Michigan Innovation Competition," Accelerate Michigan, accessed June 12, 2014, http://www.acceleratemichigan.org.

3 "For Entrepreneurs: Small Business Resources for Cities in Michigan," Gaebler Ventures, accessed June 12, 2014, http://www.gaebler.com/Resources-for-Cities-In-Mi.

4 Michigan Economic Development Corporation, accessed June 12, 2014, http://www.michiganbusiness.org/#home-intro.

5 "Global Detroit Final Report," Global Detroit, August 11, 2010, http://www.globaldetroit.com/wp-content/files_mf/1327697728Global_Detroit_Study_full_report.pdf.

6 Business Alliance for Local Living Economies (BALLE), accessed July 11, 2014, https://bealocalist.org/about-us.

From the earliest roots of civilization, food has helped define a place and its people. At the most basic level, climate and geography dictate the plants and animals that will grow, and how those food sources are acquired and eaten help to shape the culture that arises from it. Methods of growing, harvesting, preparing, and sharing foods can be as unique to a community of people as language, art, or style of dress.

Over time, the relationship between food and place has evolved into something more complex and sophisticated and less easily understood. But the basic bond remains. In viticulture, one can't discuss a wine without talking about its "terroir." An "Amish chicken" label does more than relate nutritional information; it evokes an entire value system and way of life. From Kansas City barbecue to Chicago deep dish pizza, signature foods are a powerful source of identity and shared experience.

Increasingly, people are also migrating back to the notion of local food as essential to their sense of place and to a high quality of life. In fact, today's hugely popular "foodie" culture could be partly in response to our modern disconnect from the natural ties between people and food. Just as a growing number of people are shunning the "convenience" of cars for the benefits of a walkable urban lifestyle, they are trading in the convenience of global food sourcing and industrial farming and production for a more personal and intensely social sense of belonging to a local food community. It's not a uniquely American phenomenon. In the U.K., researchers conducted a 22-year study of over 2,500 people on the meanings they attached to their food shopping experience. In 1980, "small and local" was not high on the list of criteria for choosing a food store, but by 2002 this value ranked first—even though (or perhaps because) most small local food merchants had been replaced by big box supermarkets.[1]

So how do we evaluate the economic and social impact of the local food movement on any given community? The best place to start might be by looking at the rebirth of the local farmers market, the new breed of producers and consumers who have embraced it, and the role they all play in strengthening that community's sense of place.

(ENDNOTES)

1 Ellen Desjardins, "Place and Food: A Relational Anaylsis of Personal Food Environments, Meanings of Place and Diet Quality," 29-30, Wilfrid Laurier University Theses and Dissertations, 1114, 2010.

CHAPTER PHOTO CREDITS:
MICHIGAN MUNICIPAL LEAGUE
WEBSTER'S PRIME/ALEXA TIPTON

LOCAL FOOD

A City's Journey From Field To Fork

The Local Food Movement in Kalamazoo

FOOD AS COMMUNITY BUILDER

It's a typical summer morning at Kirklin Farms, just outside Kalamazoo. Pat Smith-Kirklin is bouncing along in an electric golf cart on a well-worn garden path, headed out to the field where volunteer farmhand Nate Shaw is down on his knees and up to his elbows in heirloom tomato plants.

Shaw is a chef at Webster's Prime, an upscale dining establishment inside the Radisson Hotel in downtown Kalamazoo. For a few hours each week, he trades his white chef's coat and stainless steel knives for dirty jeans and a hoe. He's doing something that's become increasingly common in Kalamazoo's local food community: helping out a friend.

"Community is so great. Things are kind of falling apart out here, but I've had a bunch of people say they want to come out and work. What a delightful thing that is," said Smith-Kirklin. "The local food movement is very, very powerful here."

For the past 25 years, Pat Smith-Kirklin has worked alongside husband Ted on their 1,000-acre farm just down the road from where Ted grew up. She came here in 1990, fresh off a Peace Corps stint in Thailand and aching to throw her life into tending the fruits of the earth. Ted had dropped out of school in tenth grade because he couldn't stand being indoors, and had already worked his way through two wives in two hard decades of scratching out a crop farmer's living.

They were the perfect match.

"I got hooked on duck eggs in Thailand so I had to move to the country and turn into a farmer so I could start growing ducks," she joked. "I've now lived here longer than the house where I grew up. It's where my plants are, my forest. There's something so primal about it, the connection with making and using life. You're hooked into the cycle of everything."

The cart whirs silently past an overgrown peony bed shaded beneath a thick stand of mature pines—each tree once a scrawny sapling twig she'd planted there, one by one by hand, back when she first began to hone her farming skills in a tiny corner of Ted's vegetable patch. Today, most of the farm's acreage and income is still devoted to a basic Michigan field crop mix of corn, soybeans, wheat, and oats. About five acres are devoted to the specialty vegetables and cut flowers Smith-Kirklin sells at the Kalamazoo Bank Street Farmers Market and directly to local restaurants. Her produce represents less than half of one percent of the farm's production, but it now provides up to 10 percent of the gross income.

"It's gotten to the point if I absolutely had to live on the produce and had no other income, I could do it. I'd be poor, but I could do it," she said. "That's sort of an amazing thing for what began as a whim that became a passion."

But now all that is at risk. Ted, 75, has been diagnosed with a degenerative neurological disease that involves both physical decline and dementia. The couple is increasingly challenged with maintaining their operation.

"I'm taking a long, hard look at all the things we grow and trying to figure out how to simplify it and do it with a little more eye to economic rationale. We're going to have to drop a lot of the highly labor-intensive, low-profit-margin things," she said. "I can't afford to be crawling around after $6-a-pound arugula for hours on end every week

then spending more hours washing it, drying it, weighing it, fluffing it, and keeping it presentable for market. The big farms can afford to do that. I can't."

A little help from new friends like Shaw could help this family business continue to survive and even thrive. In many locales, it's unusual for a young chef to know the farmers supplying his kitchen, let alone to be out in the field lending a hand in the harvest itself. But that's no longer the case in Kalamazoo, where a vibrant local food movement has regrown the kind of deep personal ties that connect people to the food they eat, field to fork.

While difficult to translate into hard economic data, it's the kind of shift in the local culture that can help silently drive transformational change in the larger story of a city's revitalization.

"Let's be honest: right now, local sells. That's not why we do it, but it's super cool that it is a trend if that's the way we get it to come back," Shaw said. "You see it a lot in big cities. I love being part of making it a big deal here too."

It's just one example of how an agricultural trend has morphed into a placemaking phenomenon here, building a new sense of identity for visitors and residents alike, while sparking an exciting new wave of economic development within a growing sector of the Kalamazoo community.

HOW IT BEGAN

Barely a decade ago, Michigan's small family farms seemed to be going the way of the dodo, wiped out by the vast reach and efficiencies of large-scale corporate farming operations designed to feed the insatiable hunger of the fast food industry, at the sacrifice of good nutrition and environmental sustainability.

Kirklin Farms is among a growing number of small, independently owned farms that are flourishing again, thanks to a rising demand for local meats, dairy products, and produce derived from sustainable agricultural methods. In other words: good old-fashioned farming and animal husbandry, right in your own hometown.

But the roots of Kalamazoo's reinvention as a local food mecca stretch back two decades, to pioneering restaurateur Julie Stanley's opening of Food Dance in 1994.

"Local food wasn't even a model at that point. It was just a thought that the fresher produce you buy, the better it's going to taste," said Food Dance Executive Chef Robb Hammond. "As things have progressed, this whole movement has taken shape. In the process, Food Dance became the catalyst for a business model that other people have found they could use and succeed. And through our partnership with the farms, we've been able to help grow and support local farming too."

Today, Food Dance is emblematic of a vibrant local food culture that includes foodie restaurant favorites like Rustica and Zazios, and craft beer powerhouses like Bell's Brewery. But it didn't happen easily, or overnight.

"It just seemed so logical, but it was pretty unheard of at the time. At first the health department people would come in and argue with us: where'd you get that? They'd rather we bought from some commodity operation spraying with pesticides because it was familiar. So I pretty much just ignored them," Stanley said, laughing.

Hammond points to Carlson Farms in Decatur as the kind of symbiotic relationship the restaurant has nurtured with local growers. Carlson now supplies all of Food Dance's farm-fresh, antibiotic-free and hormone-free pastured chickens and eggs. ("Pastured" is the term for raising animals in a traditional pasture environment rather than the indoor enclosures of modern factory farming.) But that partnership started very simple and small.

"We have grown together, from way back in 1997 when I was just a 19-year-old prep cook who didn't know shit and we couldn't find a local supplier for eggs the way we wanted them raised," said Hammond. "Then one day Norm Carlson came in to the restaurant and said he could do it. We went out and looked at his operation and it was everything we'd hoped for."

Over a period of years, Carlson Farms gradually increased its capacity from just enough to supply half the restaurant's needs, to now supplying 100 percent of Food Dance's eggs.

"They now have a property partnership in Indiana so they can start chickens on this farm and then take them down there when they need to," said Hammond. "They've invested in their farm on no more than a handshake agreement with us that we'll buy from them and they'll sell to us. That's the kind of catalyst that is helping this whole movement grow."

THE MARKET AS COMMUNITY CORE

As local restaurants increased their interest in—and demand for—high quality local meats and produce, more and more farms of all sizes began stepping up the supply.

One of the challenges has been the physical limitations of the Kalamazoo Farmers Market itself, which has been owned and operated by the city of Kalamazoo since 1887 and is part of its parks and recreation department. It has been on its current Bank Street site since 1947.

"Everybody liked the market and wanted to have one, but nobody really wanted to invest much time or skill in nurturing it in a big way, so it's been stuck in the same small rundown structure for decades, with more vendors than space," said Smith-Kirklin. "I tried for several years to get a stall but there was no room. Then in 2002, I was able to piggyback into a space with someone who already had one, and I got to keep it when they left. But I got lucky and didn't wait in line for six years, which is what people do."

The past few seasons have seen an explosion at the market in the number of vendors, the variety of produce and products for sale, and the sheer influx of customers. According to a report compiled by city staffers in July 2013, nearly 6,000 people visit the market every Saturday in the summer, with 92 covered stalls and a courtyard of daily vendors using canopy tents.[1]

"It was this whole momentum where everybody wanted to go there, and the more people came, the more vendors wanted to be there with more things," Smith-Kirklin said. "Now it has become a very important local institution. It really is a center of community. You can feel it. It's powerful."

In 2012, results of a city survey led to proposed plans for a $1.5 million expansion to add 26 more vendor stalls and 52 more parking spaces, with larger aisles and more public space for entertainment, for a total of 188 stalls and 220 parking spaces at the same 4.12-acre site. But the plan was pushed to the back burner as the city concentrated on more pressing fiscal needs.

Meanwhile, the city has experienced a groundswell of revitalization in the neighborhood surrounding the market, particularly the The Marketplace

Project, a collaboration between the city of Kalamazoo, Kalamazoo County Land Bank Authority, and the Home Builders Association of Greater Kalamazoo. A decade ago, the Washington Square area of the city's Edison neighborhood was a rundown urban streetscape of vacant lots and abandoned buildings that had housed an adult bookstore and nude dance club. With a $15.8 million grant from the Department of Housing and Urban Development (HUD) and Michigan State Housing Development Authority (MSHDA), the group developed the seven-acre vacant parcel across from the market into a walkable neighborhood of high-quality new homes that have breathed fresh life into the city's central downtown corridor. The momentum has continued to spread in an ever-widening ripple effect of community redevelopment and economic investment.

"The market wasn't the driver to create the Marketplace neighborhood—we already owned the land and had been trying to redevelop it for years—but the market and neighborhood enhance one another," said Kalamazoo Mayor Bobby Hopewell. "It creates a central social space with major community impact. It's part of the fabric of our community."

The People's Food Co-op of Kalamazoo is now taking the market to the next level. The co-op is a consumer-owned co-operative grocery store that began during the popular natural foods movement of the late sixties and early seventies. Today, the co-op has more than 1,700 community members and is at the heart of Kalamazoo's

"The simple fact that there's so much passion around the market's fate is an indication of just how strong the local food movement has grown and how it has helped foster a new shared economy here."

organic, natural, and local foods industries. While the Kalamazoo Farmers Market is still owned by the city, the People's Food Co-op took over the actual operation in May of 2013. Under a contract valid through 2015 with three one-year renewal options, the co-op pays the city $17,000 annually and is responsible for all aspects of management including overseeing about 100 seasonal and 25 daily vendors. The co-op's Chris Broadbent was appointed as the market's full-time manager and among his responsiblities is raising funds for the proposed expansion in the city's master plan. The city continues to maintain the building and pay utility costs.

So why would a grocery store want to help boost competition from a farmers market?

"To answer that, you have to look at our mission statement. We exist to create and support access to food that's healthy for people and the economy. So we support many things like CSAs (Community Supported Agriculture) and the farmers market that in a traditional economic sense would be seen as directly in competition with us," said Co-Op General Manager Christopher Dilley.

A case in point is the 100 Mile Market. The co-op freely opens its parking lot every Wednesday to as many as 15 local vendors, some of whom also sell inside the store, but many don't. The co-op doesn't charge the vendors to be there and takes no commission off their sales. The only qualification is that they are located within 100 miles of Kalamazoo.

"I understand why some might view this as counterproductive. But it's turned out to be very financially viable for us to host that market. People come for the outside market and then come into the store for extra items, and the other way around as well. It's a win-win for everyone," said Dilley. "Everybody's talking about this concept of a new shared economy based on cooperation and collaboration rather than competition. This shows that it is working right here."

Anyone who doubts the viability of their business model need look no further than the co-op store itself, which has blossomed in size from a rundown, 784-square-foot storefront to a modern, airy building with quadruple the space. The co-op's shelves now offer close to 5,000 different items including produce, deli, meats, bulk foods, and value-added packaged goods. They welcome new local producers whenever possible.

"We do work with some national distributors, but as many local providers as we can. We pretty consistently purchase about 20 percent of our items from 70–75 local vendors," said Dilley. "What's still missing is a broader range of local items. We have a bajillion options locally for granola. It would be great if somebody was doing something not-granola."

Over at the Kalamazoo Farmers Market, positive changes were visible as soon as the "doors" opened for the 2013 season, such as prominent signs on the stalls identifying each vendor as a grower or producer, an artisan, or a broker or reseller. It has created a happy buzz among consumers and vendors alike.

"What they have done is to say this is the farmer versus just the retailer," said Webster's Prime Executive Chef Stefan Johnson. "Now if you're looking at strawberries the first two weeks of May, you know those are not Michigan strawberries. That kind of instant consumer education is a huge boost to the local food culture."

Broadbent is also working on ways to boost activity at the market beyond the Saturday crowds to Tuesdays and Thursdays. Regular vendors paid $485 per eight-foot table for the 2013 season. Daily vendors pay from $60 up to be under an awning and use electricity on a Saturday. Dilley said that there is a constant waiting list for both and the market will definitely expand and improve under the co-op's management. But how that fits with the city's master plan is yet to be determined.

"We could raze the structure there and completely replace it with a new one that, hopefully, would last another 60 years. On the flip side, we hear from some folks in the neighborhood that market days are kind of unbearable for them, and there are other neighborhoods in other parts of the city that would love to host a market as well. Everyone needs the time to have their input heard. We're hoping to have several productive, open conversations with the community before we can completely get behind a plan."

"The simple fact that there's so much passion around the market's fate, is an indication of just how strong the local food movement has grown and how it has helped foster a new shared economy here," said Dilley.

"Ten years ago, Kalamazoo was a totally different place," said Dilley. "I'm not out in the broader community hearing why people are leaving, but I sure hear a lot about people who are drawn to this community now because of how seriously we take the idea of economic development. It's not just based on the traditional economic development model, but on building a strong community based on the fundamentals like food and housing and community-based finance. That's where placemaking really takes root the strongest. I see it happening here and it's very attractive and exciting, especially to the young people. They get it that we can't keep beating the crap out of each other if we truly want to get to the next level."

AN OLD PARTNERSHIP RENEWED

If modern corporate food production can be partially blamed for the disconnect between growers and consumers, the local food movement can be credited with restoring the time-honored bond of mutual loyalty, trust, and respect once considered bedrock elements in any business relationship. But it's a relationship that has required a good deal of relearning on both sides of the equation. "You have to have dedication in the kitchen because it's a lot of work to coordinate all that," said Food Dance owner Julie Stanley. "It's getting easier for us now that we've grown our own suppliers, but I can tell you it's a challenge when you have to buy from 10 people to get enough of a couple products you need." Zazios Executive Chef John Korycki agreed. "It's really easy to become comfortable with punching an order into a computer and having it delivered the next day. Buying local means having the patience and understanding that you may or may not get it," said Korycki. "We can get angry with the big guys when it's in their catalog and you punched it in and you don't get it. But you need to be sympathetic with the farmer who just got trounced with rain for the last four days."

It also means a restaurant loses the flexibility of canceling orders at the last minute when demand suddenly changes.

"A small farm can't hold on to highly perishable produce. You cannot do that to a farmer and expect him to ever want to work with you again," said Smith-Kirklin. "John at Zazios does not screw his farmers and everybody knows it. Growers have come over to him with stuff that another restaurant had ordered and not taken, and Zazios would find a way to buy it and find a use for it. That's why if I have a limited amount of something, it goes to Zazios if they want it, first and always."

On the flip side, farmers have had to become more professional to deal with restaurants rather than just individual shoppers.

"We all felt some growing pains when it started getting bigger because some of the farmers trying to make money with everybody would short one for another," said Webster's Prime Executive Chef Stefan Johnson. "But they've gotten better at it. Most now are pretty good that if you order 25 pounds of asparagus, you get 25 pounds of asparagus. It's all part of the learning curve."

The local food movement is having a visible impact even on some of the city's most established eateries. When Johnson took over Webster's helm in 2011, the high-end, special occasion restaurant was struggling to find its way beyond conventional practices of expensive but unremarkable fare.

"My concept of food and what was on that menu were worlds apart. There wasn't a sense of ownership to what you put on the plate," said Johnson. "I wanted to impress on these young guys that somebody worked really hard to get that product to where you could purchase it so show it some respect when it gets here. There's a chain of custody to our food that we need to know."

"That philosophy is bringing Kalamazoo chefs back to fundamental culinary values that had largely been lost in the past 50 years. It is rebuilding the city's connection between food and place, and inspiring a new breed of young chefs to reinvent Kalamazoo's idea of fine dining," Johnson said.

Increasingly, local restaurants and events are basing part of their identity and marketing on this growing sense of a regional cuisine, transforming Kalamazoo into a "place" for foodies. A foodie tour and the "Fresh to You from Kalamazoo" campaign are now prominent features on www.discoverkalamazoo.com, the county's official destination marketing organization. "We're not out foraging for pine needles to cure our salmon or digging up grubs in the dirt and serving steak on moss, going crazy hyper-local like that. But we're using the tools around us to support that local environment," said Jud McMichael, a former chef now studying business at Kalamazoo Valley Community College. "Local food should be viewed as more than a trend or marketing ploy. It should be a permanent change in the way we live and do business, and how we relate to each other as a community. I dislike the word 'trend' because that implies a beginning and an end, and this should be something more than that," McMichael said. "We're a culture of convenience and our food shows that. It's about identifying factors you can change and what you can do in your daily life to move away from that, because eventually with fossil fuel depletion we're all going to be faced with it. We can choose it now or be forced into it later. Communities that choose it now will be the communities that survive in the future."

GROWING THE NEXT GENERATION

As the home of Western Michigan University, Kalamazoo helps to supply the talented workforce that fuels today's global economy. The challenge here, as elsewhere, is figuring out how to retain a share of that talent for the community's own future vitality.

Many believe the local food movement could be one of the keys to that elusive goal. The new level of creativity and excitement in the city's food service industry isn't just bringing in visitors, they say. More young people are seeing Kalamazoo as a valuable stop on their career ladder, or even the end goal itself.

Nate Shaw had originally planned to move on to Chicago or California to pursue his culinary career. But that compass bearing has changed due to his growing involvement with Kalamazoo's local food community. In the spring of 2012, the 24-year-old purchased his first home on the city's east side.

"My whole love affair with local food really started the first time that Stefan took me to the farmers market and introduced me to the growers, and told me this was part of my job now," said Shaw. "Chicago has all kinds of cool places to go and amazing opportunities to find culinary success, but my love and joy is for cooking local foods, and that's a passion I've found right here in Kalamazoo."

Korycki said that is what Kalamazoo's culinary future is all about. "It's giving these young men and women the chance to say 'this is what we think about food, this is where we're at.' Here is the next generation of producers and processors and consumers who understand it and know each other."

That same enthusiasm is visible in Kalamazoo's new breed of growers and artisans: idealistic young entrepreneurs who might just as easily have left the region to forge their dreams elsewhere.

"I look at these people starting out from scratch at age 23 and I think, God, they're brave. Some will eat dirt and live in a tent for five years," said Smith-Kirklin. "You can tell the ones who are determined enough and know what it takes. They're our future."

One such young couple is Trent and Ruthie Thompson, whose roots are in a family produce business spanning four generations and nearly 100 years in the Battle Creek area. They launched Green Gardens in 2008, producing Certified Naturally Grown vegetables, herbs, flowers, and free-range chicken eggs.

"It was family that brought me back here after spending a couple years building some farming skills out west. But it was also about better economic opportunities," said Trent Thompson, 29. "Land was more affordable here. I also felt like the market for local and organic produce was already established out west while there wasn't a lot of that going on back here in Michigan yet in 2008."

Like the urban pioneers helping to reinvent Detroit from old-school manufacturing to a technology-based economy, couples like the Thompsons are revitalizing Michigan's commodities-based farming industry with so-called "specialty" crops.

According to the 2010 Future Farmer Research Study,[2] medium-size farms in Michigan lost 300,000 acres between 1997 and 2002, mostly to suburban development and large-scale corporate operations. Thompson said that a system to better connect aspiring and existing farmers could help reverse that trend.

"A lot of farmers are getting older and need people to take over, but it's a hard thing for them to find because their own kids want to leave for other jobs, while there are lots of young people who want to farm right now. Linking them up could really be a benefit to both sides," said Thompson, who began by renting acreage, and is now transitioning to his own property. He said that knowledge and money are the two biggest challenges for beginning farmers. "This is not a lucrative business and

if you don't know what you're doing, you'll get in a deep hole really fast. We started a local growers group to help address that," said Thompson. "We basically get together once a month on a Sunday and tour each other's farms and try to help each other out by sharing knowledge and resources."

Farm incubator programs can play a critical role in helping new farmers deal with the financial challenges of land, equipment, and operating expenses, as well as provide a support network for mentorship and market contacts.

According to the National Incubator Farm Initiative, 111 farm incubator programs served 958 farmers during the 2013 growing season in the U.S. These land-based, multi-grower projects provide training and technical assistance to beginning farmers. More than half are designed to meet the needs of refugee and immigrant populations. Regional examples include the Food System Economic Partnership serving southeast Michigan. National models include the Fair Food Network. Such organizations play a key role in helping farmers find the grants and creative financing critical to their survival in a world where traditional small business loans have become difficult, if not impossible, to obtain. In the Thompsons' case, a Natural Resources Conservation Services grant funded half the $12,000 cost of one high tunnel, while another hoop house was financed with a zero-percent five-year loan from the Center for Regional Food Systems in collaboration with Michigan State University and the Fair Food Network. "We're repaying that one with vouchers distributed by the Center to low-income families in the area who then come to the market and spend the dollars at our food stand. The goal is to increase access to healthy food in inner-city 'food deserts' while helping local farmers. But low redemption rates are a problem," Thompson said. "And if people aren't using the vouchers, the farmers aren't paying down their loans."

"They're trying really hard to educate the families to use them but it's tough. They're dealing with a population that's not used to dealing with fresh food. If the rate doesn't go up at some point, we'll have to create a different plan to pay it back."

By 2013, the Thompsons were able to buy their own farm but needed to raise extra capital for a massive hoop house project that would fully transition them into a year-round operation. They used an unofficial form of crowd sourcing to fund it, well before Michigan's new crowdfunding legislation went into effect in 2014, by simply reaching out to customers and friends. "We just sent out emails to our customers outlining the project and people responded. We got all our money in a week from 11 investors on a six-year, low-interest loan. There's no way a bank would've made that loan."

Using the crowd-sourced capital, the Thompsons paid $82,000 to Ann Arbor-based Nifty Hoops to build a half-acre of high tunnels on their new farm. "Those structures will allow us to grow food all winter and increase the amount of money we're able to take in during the off-season. All that money was spent locally and employed people locally, and eventually the produce will feed people locally. And local investors will

earn the returns," said Thompson. "That's a pretty good example that this is an economic development strategy that works. It's a huge multiplier for our economy if we start growing more of our food in Michigan rather than bringing it in from China or California."

Recently, Michigan joined a growing number of states to enact investment crowdfunding legislation to make it easier for small business entrepreneurs like the Thompsons to use this creative new tool for economic development.[3]

A "PLACE" FOR FOODIES

In a relatively short time, Kalamazoo's local food movement has become an economic driver sparking an ever-widening circle of entrepreneurs in an ever-expanding array of creative ventures.

Fair Food Matters, a local nonprofit, operates the Can Do Kitchen, which allows cottage food industry entrepreneurs to use a commercial grade kitchen to create their products for sale on the open market. Kalamazoo

Valley Community College is partnering with Bronson Healthcare Group and the Kalamazoo Community Mental Health and Substance Abuse Services to create a culinary and community wellness campus focused on sustainable food production.[4]

The Kalamazoo Foods Market opened in 2010 to provide a year-round indoor venue for unique local food products that must be baked, grown, or assembled by the person actually selling the product, with resale of commercially available products strictly prohibited. The lineup currently includes Hilda's Cupcakes, granola from The Adventures of Barb and Tammy, and quiche from The Bakewell Company.

The list of seasonal markets has grown to include the Bronson Hospital Market and Douglas Farmers Market.

Tabitha Farms is an urban farm operating on two acres of land in the city's core Southside Neighborhood. It sells at the 100 Mile Market, and also has a free farm stand every Sunday where people can obtain fresh local produce.

Five new craft breweries opened in Kalamazoo in 2013 alone: Arcadia Brewing Company, Bigg Dogg Brewing, Rupert's Brew House, Tibbs Brewing, and Boatyard Brewing. City leaders helped facilitate this with a zoning change to allow microbreweries to locate in the downtown area. The result: the city placed second in the nation—right behind Grand Rapids—in the Beer City USA 2013 poll, establishing the west coast of Michigan as a nationally recognized craft beer destination.

The city also changed an ordinance that allows food trucks to operate in the downtown area. There are now many "pop-up restaurants" using trucks, trailers, and bodegas that operate throughout the city on a temporary basis.

Several city departments work cooperatively to develop new events that attract residents to parks and non-traditional venues, such as Lunchtime Live in Bronson Park every Friday from mid-July through late August. At one 2013 Lunchtime Live event, nine food trucks and vendors served hundreds of customers in Bronson Park.

The Co-Op's Dilley said there's always more to be done. "One thing we're still struggling with in Kalamazoo is the food truck piece. You hear one local grocer say bring the food trucks on, let's have them in our parking lot, it builds a reason to come to my store and strengthens what we're trying to do. But there's still a lot of anxiety on the part of restaurant owners and that pressure results in narrower policies and more stringent ordinances. Yes, food safety is a critical element we don't want to compromise on, but can we go about this in a way that supports everyone?"

Educating both the public and public officials on how such things have worked successfully in other

communities can help promote increased acceptance for healthy, positive change, Dilley said. But it's hard to know what specific policies or legislation can facilitate that proactively.

"We're all confounded by where the responsibility for different parts of this lie, and even here at the co-op we're as much prisoners of our collective understanding of how we've always done things as anybody else," Dilley said. "Sometimes it's hard to see beyond doing business as usual."

Still, "business as usual" is indeed changing in this community. Kalamazoo's placemaking success is strengthening the community with new and unexpected social benefits too.

Confections with Convictions specializes in locally hand-crafted chocolates, using young people whose criminal history has been a barrier to their efforts to find employment.[5]

Buy Local Kalamazoo is a rapidly growing network of businesses and consumers that support the local economy and enhance the unique character and integrity of the Kalamazoo area. The organization is an affiliate of the American Independent Business Alliance and includes everything from service providers to manufacturers, as long as the business is privately owned and operated, and located in the Kalamazoo area.

A host of philanthropic events, including annual gumbo and chili cook-offs, use local chefs for charity fundraising while bringing thousands of visitors to downtown.

Surplus produce from the farmers market now makes its way to local food banks at the end of each market day, providing thousands of pounds of fresh food for low-income families and the homeless.

"The folks that work in the industry of food are using their talents and abilities to impact our city in a different way," said Mayor Hopewell. "We are getting our arms around this local food piece, and you can see it everywhere in the dynamics of what's happening downtown. It is part of our masterpiece in progress, and people have grown to love us for the amazingness of what we do."

(ENDNOTES)

1 Andrea Augustine and Sean Fletcher, "Kalamazoo's Farmers Market and Local Food Movement Internal Staff Report Prepared for City of Kalamazoo," July 24, 2013.

2 Anne West, "Southeast Michigan Future Farmer Target Market Analysis," Food System Economic Partnership, August 2010, http://sepmichigan.org/wp-content/uploads/2011/09/Future-Farmer-Research-Project-3.pdf.

3 "Invest on Main Street," CrowdfundingMI, accessed July 10, 2014, http://www.crowdfundingmi.com/about.

4 Yvonne Zipp, "KVCC and Partners Will Create New Culinary Campus Focused on Food Sustainability and Wellness," Mlive.com, May 14, 2013, accessed May 12, 2014, http://mlive.com/news/kalamazoo/index.ssf/2013.05/kvcc_and_partners_to_create_ne.html.

5 Dale Anderson, "Confections with Convictions," accessed August 7, 2013, http://www.confectionswithconvictions.com.

CASE STUDY

Flint Farmers Market

Flint, Michigan — Pop. 102,434

PROJECT SCOPE

From 1905 to 1940, growers and shoppers faithfully followed the Flint City Market as it shifted locations around the downtown area three times before finally settling into a convenient site along the banks of the Flint River. For more than 73 years, the market stalls at 420 E. Boulevard Drive have been a community gathering place for generations of Flint residents and local farmers.

That cherished local tradition nearly came to an abrupt end in 2002, when the city of Flint was flat broke and going under emergency management. The historic market on the Flint River was targeted to close—it was simply costing the city too much money to operate.

That's when a group of local investors founded the nonprofit Uptown Reinvestment Corporation for the larger purpose of beginning to redevelop the entire downtown area. One of their first acts was to step in to save the market, recognizing it as an irreplaceable cultural icon in the community. Almost immediately, the new management began turning the failing gem around through local philanthropic support, creative marketing (including a name change to the Flint Farmers Market) and a series of dynamic partnerships with the community.

Today, it's a thriving hub for small independent businesses and a mecca for local foodies, as well as an important partner in many of the local and regional urban and student farming programs, including Edible Flint, Mr. Rogers Garden Project, Harvesting Earth Educational Farm, and Sanilac FFA.

From the outset, the newly reconstituted market recognized the difficult economic circumstances faced by many of its supporters and reached out to them, instituting an annual month-long educational orientation at the market for eligible participants in the federal and state Project Fresh and Senior Project Fresh food assistance programs. More recently, the market pioneered the electronic administration of the Fair Food Network's statewide Double Up Bucks program, making it even easier for low-income residents to get access to fresh, healthy foods.

In 2009, the Flint Farmers Market was voted America's Most Loved Farm Market in a nationwide poll, and was on CNN's Top Ten list of markets to visit around the country.

When Uptown was formed in 2002, a relocated downtown market had been one of the goals of its first Master Plan. By 2012, the market had become so successful it could no longer fulfill its mission at the current historic site and began actively seeking a new home. During the same time period, the city's historic newspaper, The Flint Journal, was being restructured into a mostly online entity as part of MLive, and vacated its large downtown printing facility. The Journal's decision to change its business model opened the door for Uptown's relocation goal to finally be realized. In the spring of 2014, the Flint Farmers Market moved into The Flint Journal's former print facility on First Street across from the University of Michigan-Flint campus, where it will sit squarely in the heart of the city's ongoing urban revitalization. The nationally recognized market will now have room to grow as the destination hub of an emerging regional food and health system that promotes fair food access at its core.

INVESTMENT

A $64,000 grant from the C.S. Mott Foundation allowed Uptown Reinvestment Corporation to repair electrical, heating, and plumbing systems in 2002.

• A $150,000 grant from the Ruth Mott Foundation upgraded the market's failing electric system.

• $350,000 in grants (Ruth Mott, C.S. Mott, Fair Food Network) have enabled market holders of Bridge Cards to purchase fresh fruits and vegetables for their families.

• Community partners sponsor popular events including Flower Day, Taste of the Market, cooking demonstrations, BBQ Battle, and Back to the Roots. Estimated annual value of sponsorships is $20,000.

• Relocation is part of a $28 million Health District redevelopment project which includes the demolition of Genesee Towers (a vacant bank building under serious disrepair); the redevelopment of the former Flint Journal administration building for Michigan State University's graduate program in public health and mixed-used condominiums; and the complete repurposing of The Flint Journal print facility into a public market.

SOCIOECONOMIC IMPACT

>> Currently, the market attracts 270,000 visitors a year and brings in an estimated $4–5 million for its 30–50 vendors.

>> The updated market space will provide opportunities for at least 15 new vendors; house a public meeting facility, a demonstration kitchen, two commercial kitchens to act as incubators for start-up food businesses, and an upstairs office space for health, education, or food-related businesses.

>> Provides walking distance access to healthy foods and community-centered programs and events for approximately 25,000 college students, 5,000 downtown office workers, and thousands of city residents.

>> For the past 12 years, the market has added new vendors; successfully piloted wireless bridge card incentives; created numerous partnerships; made significant building and infrastructure improvements; and created a great amount of good will and support among the area's residents. The new beautiful downtown facility will allow the market to build on the history of those accomplishments and move on to even more.

LESSONS LEARNED

>> Sometimes success requires balancing the legacy of the past against possibilities for the future, and making tough, unpopular decisions for the benefit of the larger community. Despite a fair amount of public resistance, Uptown realized the market could not continue to grow on its current historic site. The area between Burton Street and Citizens Bank was simply too small. Even if the necessary improvements were made to the market, the money would not be wisely spent because they would be improving a site which could not serve future needs. Key elements in the decision were a larger space, modern facilities that are ADA compliant, and a location downtown where residents and workers could visit much more easily.

>> Although the decision was the correct one, supporters and lovers of the old market could have been made to feel more ownership in the process.

>> Don't shy away from the media just because your project is potentially controversial. You can help lead the conversation and win public support by presenting a convincing case with solid data, and inviting the public to participate in the discussion. The original story broke on Facebook before any firm decisions had even been made, and a highly vocal, highly opinionated group of "save the market" folks emerged on social media, unintentionally spreading misinformation. "We played defense and catch-up for the first year, often not wanting to say anything publically because key decisions had not yet been made. It's made for a very interesting, rocky road, and unfortunately, it's still not over," said Flint Farmers' Market Manager Dick Ramsdell. "Sometimes success also requires balancing the power of social media to inflame and misinform against the less 'sexy' documentation of the realities of a particular situation."

>> Public/private partnerships are crucial—not just for financial contributions, but also in terms of volunteerism, social outreach, and building a strong sense of community.

Moving Placemaking Forward Through

Local Farmers Markets & Food

• In 2013, the Michigan Economic Development Corporation (MEDC) launched two new programs to facilitate local food entrepreneurship.[1] More information is available at michiganadvantage.org.

>> The Mobile Cuisine Startup Program is equipped with $100,000 to assist new or existing food truck businesses. They will provide a one-time grant of up to $10,000. There must be matching funds of at least 25 percent, a viable business plan, and the applicant must be registered to do business in Michigan.

>> The Farmers Market Grant Program is aimed at assisting existing farmers markets (operating for at least four years), making the market more accessible to residents with a one-time grant of $10,000 to $50,000. There must be matching funds of at least 50 percent.

• Michigan Public Act 100 of 2013 created a new "farmers market permit" that would allow wine sampling and sales at farmers markets, enabling small local wine makers who bottle less than 5,000 gallons of wine annually to sell their products and offer samplings at farmers markets.[2] Legislation to allow for craft beer tastings and sales at farmers markets has been introduced and is currently in the Michigan House Legislature.

• As of this writing, approximately one in five Michiganders receives food assistance. The use of Bridge Cards at farmers markets went up in Michigan by 42 percent in 2012.[3] Promoting the use of public food assistance programs at farmers markets increases sales for local growers and producers, while encouraging better public health among inner city and low income populations. Conversely, the state Department of Human Services cut 30,000 Michigan college students from the state's food stamps program in 2011.[4]

• Community Development Block Grant (CDBG) funds are available to municipalities and nonprofit organizations that operate farmers markets in non-entitlement communities. Funding is available to upgrade a market's infrastructure to operate beyond summer. Priority is given to projects that incorporate educational or entrepreneurial activities related to food.[5]

• The Passive Solar System (PSS) Loan extends seasons with funding for hoop houses, high tunnels, and unheated green houses. This technology frees growers from the constraints of a normal Michigan season, and it increases profits and provides more opportunities for

Michiganders to buy local. Interest on approved loans is fixed at 4.0 percent for a maximum of six years with interest-only payments for the first six months of the loan. Family farms, nonprofit organizations, and educational institutions are eligible to apply.[6] More information is available at michiganadvantage.org/pss.

• Food co-operatives are worker- or customer-owned businesses that aim to provide grocery items of the highest quality and best value to their members. Co-ops can take the shape of retail stores or buying clubs. All food co-ops are committed to consumer education, product quality, and member control, and usually support their local communities by selling produce grown locally by family farms. Comprehensive information on food co-ops can be found at localharvest.org.[7]

• Certified Naturally Grown (CNG) is a nonprofit organization offering peer-reviewed certification tailored to small-scale, direct-market farmers and beekeepers using natural methods. CNG was founded when the USDA National Organic Program (NOP) took effect in 2002, as an alternative to the more expensive, paperwork-intensive U.S. Department of Agriculture (USDA) program, which is geared to agribusiness and large wholesalers. The CNG program is an example of the kind of progressive policies and programs that can facilitate and support small, independent entrepreneurs. Only farmers and ranchers who support local markets and sell directly to their customers can qualify for CNG.[8]

• CulinaryIncubator.com is an online resource for small food businesses trying to find a commercial kitchen to cook their product. It enables new start-up businesses to operate without the expense of their own health department licensed commercial kitchen. The site includes a locator that currently includes 314 kitchens in its database. More information can be found at culinaryincubator.com.[9]

• Michigan Cottage Foods Law, PA 113 of 2010, exempts a "cottage food operation" from the licensing and inspection provisions of the Michigan Food Law. A cottage food operation still has to comply with the labeling and other provisions found in the Michigan Food Law, as well as other applicable state or federal laws, or local ordinances. Selling directly to consumers under the Cottage Food Law provides an opportunity for new, small scale food processors to "test the waters" and see if operating a food business is the right fit for them. The law also enables farmers who sell produce at farmers markets and farm markets to expand their product lines to include things like baked goods and jams.[10]

• The Food System Economic Partnership is a 501c3 nonprofit established in 2005 to "identify economic development opportunities and implement creative solutions to chronic issues relevant to the food system in southeast Michigan,"[11] and can serve as a model for similar local food support networks. Their Southeast Michigan Future Farmer Target Market Analysis (available on the FSEP website at fsepmichigan.org) assesses the resources, needs, and demands of aspiring and beginning farmers. While specific to counties in southeast Michigan, much of the data can be extrapolated to similar regions elsewhere.

(ENDNOTES)

1 Nikki Brown, "MEDC Creates Grant Programs for Farmers Markets and Food Trucks," Inside 208 (blog), Michigan Municipal League, June 7, 2013, http://www.blogs.mml.org/wp/inside208/2013/06/07/medc-creates-grant-programs-for-farmers-markets-and-food-trucks/.

2 "Farmer's Market Wine Permits: Bill Analysis," Senate Fiscal Agency, May 2, 2013, accessed June 11, 2013, http://www.legislature.mi.gov/documents/2013-2014/billanalysis/Senate/pdf/2013-SFA-0079-F.pdf.

3 "More People Using Bridge Cards at Farmers Markets," Stateside Staff, Michigan Radio, March 5, 2013, http://www.michiganradio.org/post/more-people-using-bridge-cards-farmers-markets.

4 Amelia Carpenter, "30,000 College Students Cut from Michigan Food Stamps Program," Michigan Radio, August 8, 2011.http://www.michiganradio.org/term/bridge-card?page=1.

5 "CDBG Farm to Food," Pure Michigan, accessed June 11, 2013, http://www.michiganadvantage.org/farm-to-food.

6 "PSS Loan Fund," Pure Michigan, accessed June 11, 2013, http://www.michiganadvantage.org/farm-to-food/.

7 "Food Co-ops," Local Harvest Inc., accessed June 11, 2013, http://www.localharvest.org/food-coops/.

8 "The Grassroots Alternative to Certified Organic," Certified Naturally Grown, accessed June 11, 2013, http://www.naturallygrown.org/.

9 "Culinary Incubator: The Source in Shared Part-Time Commercial Kitchen Rentals," Culinary Incubator, accessed June 11, 2013, http://www.culinaryincubator.com.

10 "Michigan Cottage Foods Information," Michigan Department of Agriculture & Rural Development, accessed June 11, 2013, http://www.michigan.gov/mda rd/0,4610,7-125-50772_45851-240577-,00.html.

11 "About," Food System Economic Partnership, accessed July 17, 2013, http://fsepmichigan.org/index.php/about/.

Mardi Gras and New Orleans. Carnival and Rio de Janeiro. Burning Man and Nevada's Black Rock Desert.

Sometimes it isn't the actual city or physical space that draws people to a place. It can be an event that is so unique, so iconic, that it becomes synonymous with the geographic point where it happens.

Interestingly enough, while these events are usually expressions of art and culture, they're rarely the product of our formal arts and cultural institutions. These iconic special events are often the result of years of dedicated effort by countless numbers of passionate organizers and participants.

That phenomenon is one of the lessons that planners, community development experts, and local leaders are now learning about creative placemaking.

From the Project for Public Spaces, a nonprofit, planning, design, and educational organization dedicated to helping people create and sustain public spaces that build stronger communities, "Why do these cultural centers physically remove culture from the public realm and plop it on a curated, often 'visionary' pedestal instead of providing a venue for promoting more interaction among the people who create it? 'Big Cultural Centers–think of Lincoln Center in Manhattan–they need to turn themselves inside-out and become about culture for all instead of culture for a few,' says PPS CEO Fred Kent. 'Elitism is a big part of what's going on in some of these places. They exude a subtle sense of who 'should' and 'should not' be there.'"[1]

Special events are one way to do that, bringing arts and culture out to the streets–literally–and into the hearts and minds of the people, where they can be shared and celebrated by all.

(ENDNOTES)

1 "Creativity & Placemaking: Building Inspiring Centers of Culture," Project for Public Spaces, August 16, 2012, accessed March 14, 2014, http://www.pps.org/reference/creativity-placemaking-building-inspiring-centers-of-culture/.

SPECIAL EVENTS

a foolish idea

Bringing Random Art to the Streets of Ann Arbor

Imagine a city street that's come to life with bizarre and fanciful dreams, plucked like magic from the minds of its citizens. Children stroll along in the dark with brightly colored glowing fish bobbing above their heads. A giant angry ice cream cone chases its sweet-toothed eaters with a cartoon baseball bat. Alice's White Rabbit bobbles his head above a Salvador Dali clock, while an army of tiny toy robots march in mechanical step with shiny CD eyes.

It's April Fools in Ann Arbor: the one place to be for the Foolish, on a day unlike any other, anywhere else on earth.

As far back as the Roman festival of "Hilaria" and the Medieval "Feast of Fools," people have made mischief and merriment a cause for celebration. While no one is certain of its actual origins – it might have been Chaucer's Canterbury Tales -- the first of April somehow became the official date for practical jokes and playful pranks, hijinks and shenanigans.

But until now, no one has laid claim to this oddest of holidays. There are no Hallmark cards to commemorate it, no formal rituals to observe it, no particular place to be when the madness and mayhem begin.

That is, until a University of Michigan art teacher came up with a Foolish idea.

AN ARTIST'S EYE

Mark Tucker grew up in Rutland, Vermont. But instead of hiking and skiing the Green Mountains, he amused himself by riding a unicycle, juggling, and performing magic and ventriloquism. After receiving his Bachelor of Fine Arts degree in Art at Ohio Wesleyan University and a Master of Fine Arts in Painting at the University of Michigan, Tucker began his artistic career by answering a blind ad to build parade floats for the Michigan Thanksgiving Parade, a major and time-honored event which takes place each fall on Woodward Avenue in downtown Detroit. While serving as the parade's art director, Tucker traveled to Europe to learn the fine art of carta pesta (papier-mâché) from the world famous float builders of Viareggio, Italy.[1]

In Viareggio, the tradition of a carnival celebration with floats began with a parade on Shrove Tuesday in 1873. The massive floats for the annual carnival were originally built by Viareggio's ship builders: highly skilled carpenters and iron workers whose renowned and rugged ships were made to sail the world's high seas. In 1925, papier-mâché replaced the original shipbuilding materials. As a result, the still-strong but now lightweight floats became even larger and more elaborate. Some reach as high as the rooftops of the five-story buildings lining the streets of the parade, with moving parts and puppets manipulated by people inside the float using an ingenious system of weights and levers. Today's floats are planned and worked on year-round, with the papier-mâché puppets satirizing public and political figures and topical news events. The largest floats can carry as many as 200 costumed people dancing, singing, and throwing confetti.[2]

Tucker later moved to Boston and worked as a

freelance scenic painter for ten years, painting sets for opera, ballet, television, TV commercials, and movies. When he returned to Michigan with his wife and three sons, he began teaching art to mostly non-art majors within the Lloyd Hall Scholars Program (LHSP) at the University of Michigan. LHSP is a living-learning program focused on writing and the arts, where first- and second-year students live in a close-knit community together, and take small writing and studio arts classes with highly specialized faculty. Events are an intrinsic part of the experience: photography exhibits, theater performances, live concerts, even poetry slams. The program is built on the premise that learning and living together encourages personal and intellectual development.[3]

In 2006, Tucker was searching for a novel way to bring his LHSP students together with community members to create something unique and exciting for his "Art in Public Spaces" course. The result was the Street Theater Art (START) Project.

"What one course do you teach if that is going to be their only art course? That became the challenge," said Tucker. "I was teaching drawing and painting for these non-art majors but I didn't feel comfortable. It didn't seem like enough. These people are going to go out and be the movers and shakers in the world. I wanted them to feel and understand the impact that arts can have in a community."

As serendipity would have it, at about the same time Tucker was helping a friend design sets for a neighborhood theater group, the Burns Park Players.

"We were doing Fiddler on the Roof and we made these two puppets that came down the aisle for the dream sequence. So the ghost of Fruma-Sarah came down and she was so scary that kids ran out of the theater, including my own three-year-old," said Tucker,

laughing. "Then we got to thinking that wow, this was really effective. Okay, what would 50 of these puppets look like on the street instead of two in the theater?"

Just a few years earlier, theater director Julie Taymor had blown away Broadway audiences with the innovative costume designs for the theatrical version of The Lion King. The incredible life-size animal puppets of The War Horse were also in the process of being born.

All those things began to come together in Tucker's imagination.

"There had been this reemergence of puppetry as a legitimate theatrical pursuit. So what would happen if we had a whole class of students who made these giant puppets that were too big for them to actually complete themselves, so they would require community help? We'd have this community engagement aspect built right into the piece."

The idea became the first START project: a student puppet-making workshop assisted by community volunteers which would culminate at the semester's end with a public celebration in downtown Ann Arbor. To make it happen, he teamed up with then-graduate student Shoshana Hurand, a former LHSP student who was equally excited at the prospect of a hands-on public art project. They started with a class of 20 non-art majors, and invited in any community members interested in taking part in their creative venture.

"We decided to call it FestiFools because April Fools' Day just happened to work with the academic calendar as the end of the semester," said Tucker.

That first year was little more than an act of inspired and orchestrated chaos.

"We sort of just did it. We didn't go and get all the right permissions in all the right ways at first. We just rented a garage down on Felch Street. Someone from OSHA found out about us because a student had called them trying to get a free first aid kit for us. They came and saw our setup which was cold water, no sump pump, no bathrooms for the students. Voilà, the next year the university moved us into here," said Tucker, grinning impishly as he gestured around at the 2,500-square-foot workspace that now houses the FestiFools studio inside a campus warehouse.

The next step was finding a place to stage the performance itself. What better venue for street theater than Main Street USA? Tucker approached two city council members who were part of his Burns Park neighborhood theater group.

"We were very fortunate with the city of Ann Arbor. I lived in Boston for 10 years and I thought I knew what community was, but then we moved here into the Burns Park neighborhood and I started helping out with the theater and suddenly I know and I mean know 100 people that I've spent time arguing and crying and laughing and partying with. Two of them happened to be on the city council."

They encouraged him to start by seeking the support of the downtown business community.

"We talked with the Main Street Area Association, the Chamber of Commerce, the Convention and Visitors Bureau. We went to all of these business association meetings and stuff, getting up there trying to explain this thing that was still pretty much just an idea on a napkin. We didn't really even know if we could deliver what we were saying we were going to deliver."

But one business owner, Dennis Serras of Main Street Ventures, offered more than just his okay for a Main Street event.

"He gave us our first $1,000 check and I thought this is going to be easy. All of them are just going to write $1,000 checks and all we need are 20 of these and we'll be on our way," said Tucker, shaking his head and laughing. "It was the last $1,000 we saw for quite some time other than some in-kind stuff."

Ann Arbor City Council Member Margie Teall, and Main Street Area Association leads Ellie Serras and Maura Thomson, were also among those first visionaries who saw the potential of Tucker's Foolish idea.

"The contributions of private citizens have played an even more important role," said Tucker. "Even with support from the business community, getting a project like FestiFools off the ground and keeping it afloat, year and year after, often boils down to the generosity of just a handful of private citizens. Sometimes, even just one dedicated supporter can make all the difference."

"We really couldn't have done any of this without the tremendous support of our angel donors, Jeri Rosenberg and Vic Strecher. From day one, their ongoing support has been our financial rock that's made it possible for us to do this in the first place," said Tucker. "Vic and Jeri have contributed well over $100k just to keep us afloat, and they offered and have sustained an annual pledge to us even before we received any other funding. It would be disingenuous for us to suggest that we accomplish what we do on a sustained level without folks understanding that we've been very lucky to have these two really dedicated, unbelievably generous supporters in our pocket."

At this point, they now had in hand the necessary approvals from the city and downtown businesses, and solid financial backing from the

community. They were ready to get the project started.

But in order to get enough puppets to actually make the event work, Tucker also needed a bigger workforce than he had at hand. He quickly engaged Nick Tobier, a friend and associate professor at the University of Michigan Stamps School of Art and Design, who offered to bring in 150 freshmen from a class focused on art history and social consciousness.

"Instead of doing a final exam with them, for two weeks he'd group these students into smaller groups and they each would make a puppet at their own facility up on North Campus. So along with the 25 puppets we were making, he was bringing another 25 or so," said Tucker. "Just in terms of the scale of the street we needed a certain critical mass of these just to make it work. But it was also the theater of it. They didn't know what we were making and we didn't know what they were making. It's pretty amazing to see the way the puppets interact when they see each other for the first time out there on the street. It's like puppet love or puppet hate."

Another Stamps professor, Holly Hughes, also joined in with her students, along with Kelly Quinn's College of Urban Planning students.

On April 1, 2007, the first FestiFools burst onto Main Street in downtown Ann Arbor with a colorful army of huge papier-mâché creations, the cumulative effort of more than 200 students and countless community members, to the amazed delight of hundreds of spectators lining the street. It was unlike anything any of them had ever seen.

Among them was Shary Brown, who was then the executive director of the original Ann Arbor Street Art Fair, established in 1960 as the first of what is now a group of four award-winning art fairs taking place together each summer in Ann Arbor.

"That first year my husband and I got there more than an hour early because I was so excited and wanted to be sure we got a front row spot," said Brown. "I just fell in love with it. It was an art event that was so freshly Ann Arbor."

Brown wasn't the only fan. The first FestiFools event was enthusiastically praised by the Ann Arbor News editorial board, and Mayor John Hieftje presented FestiFools with a Golden Paintbrush Award for excellence in public art, with the promise that FestiFools would return in 2008 as an annual Ann Arbor tradition.

When Tucker heard Brown was retiring from the art fair, he immediately called to recruit her expert help to keep his new event going beyond that first year. He didn't have to ask twice.

"It was a perfect linkage to have had the honor of the stewardship of what is really an Ann Arbor signature event, and then to be invited to join this whole new take on a community art event," said Brown.

She was also drawn to the exciting feeling of "spontaneous combustion" that surrounded FestiFools.

"It's the community-built part of it. Our responsibility as organizers is to provide the platform. We create the stage. If you contrast it with events like the art fairs or summer festival, it's the same concept of public art, but they're curated productions and this is community built, inspired and created. We literally don't know what we're going to get until it comes."

Still, it's not as random and rogue an event as it might appear on the surface.

"Here in Ann Arbor we're a highly educated community and our curated events are really top notch. So there's an expectation of quality that I think also translates to FestiFools," said Brown. "Plus there's been a community engagement component since the beginning. That's what the studio community time has done. There's a real attitude of community investment in it."

BEYOND THE MERRIMENT

Thanks to all those factors, that original Foolish idea has blossomed in wonderful and unexpected ways over the past seven years. One of those has been Fools in Schools, a unique form of educational outreach that brings arts enrichment to underserved youth populations in inner city schools.

"We have this great resource here which is called college students. So we took 15 of them a few years ago and we worked in two elementary schools in Detroit," said Tucker. "We worked on a mini FestiFools project with the kids. The idea was they could create it however they wanted, it could be about whatever they wanted, they could have it on whatever day they wanted, but it had to involve the kids and their caregivers and community folks."

"These schools hadn't had arts programming for six or seven years at that point. The idea was at least we could start an event and if they liked it, then maybe, just maybe—just the same way we have to keep making this thing every year whether we want to or not—then maybe that would happen there and then they would have to have some arts programming in their schools even if it wasn't mandated by Detroit Public Schools."

It was also meant to be an enrichment experience for the college students, funded by a University of Michigan program called Global Intercultural Experience for Undergraduates (GIEU).

"The idea is for students to go out into the world. Well, we could go 45 minutes away and be out in the world," said Tucker. "But I didn't want our students at five o'clock to be able to say 'ok I can go home now.' So we brought our sleeping bags and lived there, stayed right there in the building for 10 days, ate the lunch and reduced price breakfast right along with the kids. They never had anyone do that before. It cost us $20,000 just to pay for security. That was the only way they were going to let us do that."

Immediately after the Detroit experience, Tucker took the same group of students to a small rural town in northern Italy, where they spent the next three weeks working in a similar program started by a group from New York City's Village Halloween Parade, an annual event which draws an estimated two million visitors to the city's Greenwich Village each October 31st.

"The people had essentially abandoned this town a mile up in the Alps so it was like four people in the winter and in the summer it swelled to maybe 20. So we knew we could do a lot."

Besides helping them with the festival project,

the students worked to clear hiking trails and helped in the annual harvest of an alpine flower used to make a special local liqueur.

"It was similar issues, similar problems, but different communities completely. There, you had schools really depressed because everyone was moving out of the rural areas, so you didn't have enough students to keep the schools alive and people had to take their kids two hours away. It was all these sorts of interesting parallels going on, so it was really powerful."

Today, the little Alpine village's annual festival has helped make it a popular agritourism destination for hikers and cyclists, and many of its former inhabitants are now reclaiming their ancestral homes as summer places or vacation rentals.

The Village Halloween Parade group now also comes to Ann Arbor each March to help out in the FestiFools studios.

"They have been working with their parade for 20 years so this is their craft, this is their business, this is what they know how to do. So some of the techniques we use we learned from them," said Tucker. "It's a great partnership."

Sadly, the Detroit elementary school where the students worked has since burnt down, with students and staff dispersed to other schools. But Tucker hopes to get another grant to do a similar educational outreach project next year.

"That's the great thing about it all. Before I was teaching a drawing and painting class and students were putting their stuff in their little drawers or taking them home. This way they spend weeks on making something, and then they give it up. We hang it up here and they give it up to the community by going out and performing it that day for one hour. And we've never produced a professional puppet maker from this class, you know what I mean? So what is the intrinsic value of this? At the end they have to write a paper where they have to reflect on that. Why did I take this class? What am I learning here?"

Beth Johnson, an art history major, is one of the students in the 2014 FestiFools class.

"Growing up in Ann Arbor, I've always been interested in public art and community art events. Being in the class allows me to be a part of putting on an event that is really special," said Johnson. "I'm interested in bringing the community and university together both as a member of the Ann Arbor community and as a student. It's a reminder that we are in the community of Ann Arbor, not just on our own little island campus."

BY THE LIGHT OF THE MOON

By 2011, FestiFools had become so popular that a second event was added: FoolMoon, a nighttime luminary festival that takes place on the Friday night immediately before the Sunday FestiFools celebration.

The idea began when Tucker's crew was asked to create lighted paper sculptures for a local production of Peter and the Wolf. The commissioned project fell through, but the unused luminaries sparked another brilliantly Foolish idea.

"We thought 'Let's just not just trash it. They're so much fun to make, don't you think people in the community would want to make them?' Because we got all kinds of calls from people wanting to make the papier-mâché puppets and they do come help us do that. But they really want to make their own and they don't realize these things take two months to make. The luminaries

"I like the free-form nature of this parade, the carnival-esque way that it includes the crowd. It's like a moving collage... it empowers the artist and it empowers the audience."

are much simpler with smaller materials and less of an investment time-wise. Of course, some people do put a tremendous amount of time and imagination into these too, but you don't have to. You could walk away two or three hours later with one of these. So the entry point is a little more do-able."

They hired Michigan Thanksgiving Parade float designer Jimmie Thompson to oversee the free luminary workshops held each Sunday in March leading up to the event. "The workshops are an integral part of the shared public art experience", said Tucker.

"There's this whole culture and life that goes on in the process of this. The two events combined are just a few hours long but it is the process leading up that is the real meat holding it together. We recognized that the community wanted not just to make something at their house but to work with people who knew how to make things. So what we did was create these community workshops with artists to teach and help people build their own luminaries," said Tucker. "I'd have Jimmie here every day if I could afford it. You can't underestimate the value that professional artists bring. As much as you can do with volunteers and students, you have to have some people who actually can come in and teach others. But that is a luxury. This time I got a grant from the university to get him here a month early so we're back in the game again. That's the way it is every year: one more year of scrappy funding to see if we can do it again."

For Thompson, FestiFools and FoolMoon provide a fun change of pace from his regular job working in the more traditional style of a large-scale commercial event like the Michigan Thanksgiving Parade.

"I like the free-form nature of this parade, the carnival-esque way that it includes the crowd in. It's like a moving collage, things coming up and moving in from all over the place, rather than that traditional military line down the street," said Thompson. "It empowers the artist and it empowers the audience."

The free luminary workshop space is provided by Workantile, a nontraditional work community located inside a remodeled storefront on Main Street in downtown Ann Arbor.

An outgrowth of the new "shared economy" culture, Workantile is an innovative shared workspace for independent, self-employed workers whose membership dues allow them to work in a social setting within an attractive, professional environment they probably couldn't have afforded on their own. Opening their space to community events like the FoolMoon luminary workshops is part of Workantile's mission as a member of the downtown business community.

"It's turned out to be a very positive, mutually beneficial relationship that has allowed FestiFools access to a temporary space that already exists in the community", said Brown.

"It's a terrifically interesting group of people who don't use their space much on Sundays and, at the same time, we provide some visibility for them by bringing in a lot of people who might never have heard about them otherwise. So it meets some of their needs and our needs at the same time," she said.

The workshops are a happy mass of organized madness, like an adult-sized kindergarten art class. Men, women, teens and kids all crowd the long work tables side by side, up to their elbows in mounds of wire and packing tape, fashioning giant wire-and-cellophane lovebirds and butterflies, unicorns and stars. Up in the front window, others are busily slopping white craft glue onto their constructions, then covering them with scraps of colored tissue paper. Some of the workers have even spilled out onto the sidewalk, hanging their creations to dry from the light poles and bike racks outside.

One of them is Eric Bassey, a professional event producer and database developer who's created a giant rabbit for this year's "moonagerie" theme.

"A lot of my adult life I've spent working in the arts, primarily theater, so I really like the theatricality of it. It really takes performance and art out of the gallery and theater and into the open, out on the street where everybody can see it without going out of their way. It is truly art in a public space," said Bassey. "Things like FestiFools and FoolMoon are really giving the impetus back to art for art's sake. It makes life more enjoyable and vibrant. Ann Arbor is definitely one of the communities willing to lead in that direction, among places like Austin and San Francisco and Madison, Wisconsin."

Bassey, 44, grew up in Michigan but went to school and lived in New York until 1991. Ann Arbor's reputation as a center for arts and culture was the main reason he chose to relocate there, he said.

"When I moved here I didn't have a particular field yet to claim as my own, so I had the ability to pick a place where I wanted to be and where I knew people, which was another primary draw," he said. "FestiFools and FoolMoon have become part of the cultural identity of the city. That really becomes an attractive element. People know this is something that happens in this city, and that makes this city a more attractive and interesting place to live. It really has the potential to draw people who are able to take into consideration these types of things when making a choice."

FoolMoon was an instant hit, engaging people of all ages in an eclectic, electric community art pageant that has in some ways become even bigger than the

original Sunday spectacle. After weeks of preparation in the public workshops, the moonlight event starts in the late afternoon at the Grizzly Peak Brew tent with live music and FoolBrew, the event's signature beer. As the sun sets, the merrymakers head to one of three official starting points around the city core. The enormous processions of hand-made illuminated sculptures thread their way along the streets to coalesce in the heart of downtown Ann Arbor, where the merriment continues with candlelit treats, shimmering shadow puppet performances, innovative music, building-sized experimental film projections, and more.

"The crazy thing about it is it's really 99% community built," said Tucker. "We thought it was just going to be an adult event because it happens after dark. But people bring their kids and they all stay until 11 at night."

FoolMoon also fills a critical economic need for the group. As the project has grown increasingly into a public endeavor and the university's administrative and financial support has diminished, Tucker's band of merrymakers have had to explore new ways to keep the concept financially viable.

"We needed to raise funds to keep going with this, but we didn't want to sell out FestiFools. Part of its charm and allure, whether people realize it or not, is that it's completely commercial free," said Tucker. "If you want to do something political that's fine but you can't do it on a sign. We will come out and reeducate you on that day. We don't want people handing out stuff, we don't want companies coming and saying 'I'll put my name on this one, not that one.' So we started FoolMoon saying this will be our event that brings in the money that supports both the events."

Even so, FoolMoon hasn't compromised their artistic integrity. In fact, just the opposite: it's challenged them to come up with advertising methods that are true to the aesthetics of the event.

"We found clever ways and are always looking for new clever ways to show off our sponsors where it's not just hanging up a banner," said Tucker. "Like we make these little gobo lanterns where we cut out their name and my students will run around and shine them on buildings and people and stuff like a little Batman Bat-Signal."

A WONDERFOOL FUTURE

WonderFool Productions became a registered Michigan nonprofit in December of 2012 and applied for 501c3 status in June of 2013. The group's nonprofit status was officially accepted by the Internal Revenue Service in June of 2014.

"We can't overemphasize the importance of the role the university has played in starting this event as a university course, and providing a lot of the administrative support services that we're now taking over," said Brown. "Now we're growing into a new phase. Our progress into the future would be more rapid if we had fulltime staff. We're still largely volunteer-driven which is wonderful but it's also inefficient when you are relying on people to juggle their lives and priorities to make sure their volunteer commitments rise to a priority in their lives, and the 10,000 are going to come whether you're ready or not."

For 2014, the group was able to hire a part-time administrative assistant to perform vital but time-consuming tasks like getting bids on sound and power equipment for FoolMoon's deejay display, and ordering the event tee shirts that generate a significant share of funds each year.

Community involvement goes far beyond the individuals who show up on weekends to help out in the studio. It also takes an army of local organizations and businesses that have joined in the enthusiastically supportive fray in various ways.

"As we develop this, we're finding so many Ann Arbor businesses and institutions who recognize what we're trying to achieve and are supporting us in some way or another," said Brown. "It's not just 'here's our product if you can use it.' It's 'what do you need to make it work?' There are all kinds and they've brought things of real value to us."

Some are core business sponsors, like Ace Barnes Hardware which helps source cost-effective materials, and the owners of Grizzly Peak Brew Pub, who host the beer tent during the FoolMoon celebration and also donate proceeds from their FoolBrew that is served at several local restaurants as a fundraiser.

The Ann Arbor District Library has been an important community partner almost since the beginning, working with young library patrons to build handmade robot costumes to expand the festivities, offering free use of equipment and workspace, and sharing its network of highly-skilled tech people to bring new creative elements to the events.

"For example, they have a group of very differently talented film and tech people who've programmed and created interactive projections on the sides of buildings that we use during FoolMoon, and the library has this enormous projector that enables us to get the building-size projections," said Brown. "Having access to that kind of technical talent and equipment to use for four hours a year is amazing. That's not something you can easily find in every community."

As WonderFool Productions continues to grow, new challenges also continue to arise.

For example, the seven-year relationship with the Stamps students ended this year when the class was moved to the fall semester in 2014.

"That was a huge loss for us, 150 students that were making 25 pieces on North Campus. We'll miss that," said Tucker, who is scrambling to make up the loss by scavenging parts from past puppets hanging in the studio rafters. "Up until this year, the idea was to never bring out a puppet twice. Part of the magic is if you don't come, you don't see it and the next year it's going to be all new. But this year we're in emergency mode so we're pulling down some of the old ones to retrofit."

Thankfully, other puppet "recruits" are starting to show up to fill out the ranks as the event's fame slowly spreads.

"I'd say maybe 30 percent now is folks coming from other places. We've had calls this year from a group in Syracuse, New York, and there's always a group from Toledo, and another from southern Indiana. So that's a trend we hope grows because it makes our job easier. We just put on the event and they come," said Tucker.

"So far, 'quality control' hasn't been a problem," Tucker said.

"They see our stuff online or have come to past events and get the aesthetic of it. It's hard to tell now what's theirs and what's ours. But it's a balancing act. I personally don't want it to devolve into a Halloween parade with the goofy hat you bought at Target. I really want it to be about handmade art. I don't care how badly handmade but I want you to have invested something in it. And hopefully, we'll have different artists come in and raise the bar so that there is always a striving for quality rather than dumbing down the event."

WonderFool Productions' five-member board

recently defined a three-pronged mission that is raising the bar on their own ambitions for the future: educational outreach, community engagement, and the establishment of a physical space that could become a shared creativity center for many local community groups.

"One of the benefits in having a small board, particularly at the beginning of an organization when you're planning for the future, is that our communication is finer tuned. It's easier to get us together and make time commitments to do the planning we need to do," said Brown. "We've got some very thoughtful people in this group with disparate skills with just enough cohesion. So last year we took a look at the future together over a two-day period, and we came up with these three initiatives or goals that we thought were possible and plausible."

Fools in Schools will hopefully, continue the work that Tucker started in 2010 in Detroit, and perhaps eventually expand into other school systems around the state.

"We really want to get in at the system level but we're too small. We haven't proved ourselves. We think we know we could do something exciting but we don't have that 10 years of data and proof yet to go into a school system. So we're doing this ad hoc, one school, one art teacher, one principal at a time, and that's exhausting," said Tucker. "But for me, it's a creative quest and it's an educational tool like none other."

In 2013, they expanded their community engagement efforts beyond Ann Arbor, taking a version of FoolMoon to ArtPrize[4] in Grand Rapids.

This year they've been invited back to host luminary workshops during ArtPrize 2014.

"If creativity is the core of what we do, there are many ways to support and encourage creativity in others," said Brown.

"ArtPrize is just a first step in that process", said Tucker.

"We are testing out if this really is an event we could package and put in a box and send to a small town that is trying to revitalize. Is there a way that we could make this not very expensive for them to do, cost-effective for us to put together, and maybe still benefit our nonprofit so we could then keep doing these things for other towns? We know we've just hit the tip of the iceberg."

But financing all that continues to be a challenge.

"If you include some of the in-kind things we'd have to pay for if they were not donated, I think you could look at about $60,000 bare bones to do this, not including the building space, which the university has provided," said Brown. "As we evolve away from the university, one of the huge pieces we will need to provide ourselves is studio space. One of the things we'll have to do over time is figure out maybe some nontraditional ways to find and use space."

Still, even with all its popularity and ever-growing fame, the future for FestiFools is not guaranteed, especially as the university's support role diminishes.

"That's why we started the nonprofit. If we don't build another ship to put this on in the community, I can see this not happening in a year or two. That's how quickly things can change," said Tucker. "But we're going to figure this thing out, we're going to come up with creative solutions. That's part and parcel of doing this thing. It's just like the weather. It's going to be great that day or it's going to be lousy, and we're still going to be out there doing it."

And in a perfect world where anything is possible? Tucker points to Viareggio, Italy, and the festival where he found his initial inspiration.

Each February, hundreds of thousands of visitors from all over the world flock to the tiny seaside resort town, packing the streets as far as the eye can see around the incredible spectacle that is Carnevale di Viareggio.

"Here, everyone comes to our free event and we're picking on the same nice businesses and the same nice people who are giving so much year after year and maybe not getting that much back out of it. Viareggio would be the other model, where they close off all the streets and all these people have paid 20 Euros to get in. But that's what's afforded them to create an event unlike anything we've ever seen in the United States, and it's allowed for a whole culture of artists who've moved there to work on these year-round and who get paid just like your dentist gets paid. And this is a town that's no bigger than Ann Arbor, probably smaller. We could have that kind of thing here 130 years from now. But that's a vision that takes a lot of people coming together."

He's not the only one to see the potential. The Ann Arbor Convention and Visitors Bureau features both events prominently on its website and in its marketing materials as two of the city's signature events and tourist attractions.

"They would love for this to be a whole weekend event. Right now we've got FoolMoon on Friday night and FestiFools on Sunday so we've got these two pieces of bread but we've never put the filling inside. But it becomes a problem of scale and funding at that point just to add one more event on Saturday. We just can't ask the same funders and volunteers over and over to do all this work. So it's really challenging."

But for now, in this particular place and time, this band of merrymakers is happy just to keep doing what they've learned to do best: making art into a living, breathing communal experience that can be shared by literally everyone.

And what advice would Tucker give to anyone else seeking to replicate his Foolish idea?

"To be honest, if I had realized everything that goes on behind the scenes I don't know that I would have started. And with the way the economy went, I think if we'd started it a year later it wouldn't have gotten off the ground. I don't think there would've been the support. So we were lucky," said Tucker. "But now with social media so much better than it was eight years ago, you can essentially just do something like this.

"I would say just find a place that's not illegal to do it and do not go get too much permission beforehand. I can't tell you how many people we tried to explain to them what we were going to do, and scared more of them than we convinced.

"Just do it. People will see it and love it. And then you can keep on doing it."

(ENDNOTES)

1 "FestiFools: Our Story," WonderFool Productions, accessed March 10, 2014, http://FestiFools.org/about-us/.

2 "Viareggio Carnival," Understanding Italy, accessed March 10, 2014, http://www.understandingitaly.com/tuscany-content/viareggio-carnival.html.

3 "About Us," Lloyd Hall Scholars Program, accessed March 10, 2014, http://www.lsa.umich.edu/hsp/aboutus.

4 "Art Prize," accessed June 10, 2014, http://www.artprize.org.

CASE STUDY

Marche du Nain Rouge

Detroit, Michigan — Pop. 713,777

PROJECT SCOPE

The first Marche du Nain Rouge started with an intriguingly simple question: "What would Detroit's version of Mardi Gras look like if it happened today?" Detroit is actually older than New Orleans, has some of the same traditions of great roots, music, and culture, and was also founded by the French. The city's name originates from the French phrase le détroit du lac Érié, or the strait of Lake Erie, which links Lake Huron and Lake Erie.[1] But unlike its southernmost French cousin, the tradition of Mardi Gras never really took hold in Detroit.

So in the fall of 2009, a small group of Detroiters decided to change all that, and began to plan the city's first bona fide Mardi Gras celebration, to be held in March 2010.

Of course, the Marche du Nain Rouge is not Mardi Gras, but it is designed to have some of the same feel, using art, culture, history, and creative expression to give folks a reason to rejoice in the spring and let loose.

The Nain Rouge (Red Dwarf or Red Gnome in French) is entrenched in 300 years of Detroit urban legend. The Nain was said to have bumped heads with Detroit's first white settler, Antoine de la Mothe Cadillac, back in 1701. Cadillac lost his fortune and died penniless back home in France. Forever after, the Nain was said to have appeared at various times in the city's history as a harbinger of bad fortune. So each spring, Detroiters celebrate the season and the city's rebirth by banishing the evil spirit from the city for another year. Parade participants and spectators are encouraged to wear costumes so that when the Nain Rouge next returns, he will not recognize the people who once again ousted him from the city limits, and thus will not be able to seek personal vengeance.[2]

The Marche itself lasts about 90 minutes, beginning in Midtown near Wayne State University, and parades about a mile through the area known as the Lower Cass Corridor, which centers on Cass Avenue, running parallel with Woodward Avenue, a main Detroit artery running north towards suburban neighborhoods. The route ends at Cass Park (a U.S. Historic district in Midtown) and the Masonic Temple (the world's largest Masonic temple, built in 1922). The Nain appears at the beginning to taunt Detroiters, then challenges them to follow him to Cass Park, where he performs another ritual round of raucous taunting before the celebrants rise up against him and he disappears for another year.

The Marche du Nain Rouge has grown over the course of the past five years. The first year, the founders were just surprised people came out for such a crazy thing. The second year, they secured Cass Park again, but expanded the scope of the offerings to include vendors and staged music. Since the third year, they have shifted the opening ceremony to a larger parking lot and have ended at the Masonic Temple, right across from Cass Park, in order to accommodate the growing crowd.

From the start, the one-day festival/parade has been shepherded by a small planning committee of essentially the same core group of 6–10 people, who begin planning each fall for the next spring's event.

Over the last several years, they have also worked to expand partner events. For the last two years, Tour deTroit[3] has offered the Run du Nain Rouge, a costumed 5K fun run that immediately precedes the Marche. In 2014, Eagle Rock Yacht Club hosted a Nain Rouge dodgeball tournament to benefit a local recreation center. Since the second year, they have worked with a variety of small businesses, both as sponsors

and as partners, to develop and promote events and merchandise that are Nain Rouge themed to help grow the event into more of an extended festival.

In a very short span of time, the event has become an iconic symbol of Detroit's growing allure as a post-industrial age phoenix and a mecca for those seeking a vibrant and creative urban lifestyle, and the chance to help make the city's future whatever they choose. The 2013 Marche even caught the eye of The Huffington Post, which lauded the festival's placemaking power by playfully asserting that "centuries from now, historians will sing the praises of the brave…Detroiters who swarmed the Cass Corridor last Sunday in legion to banish the Nain Rouge away once again."[4]

INVESTMENT

>> The first Marche cost about $1,000, which came completely out of the planners' pockets to pay for the city's fire and parade permits and for costumes and props. About 250 people showed up.

>> By the second year, the costs had grown along with the festival itself. Planning begins in the prior fall, when the first permit application goes to the city. As of 2014, the committee has decided to start meeting throughout the year.

>> An event chair is appointed to be a main point of communication between the committee, the city, and the various other interested parties. This chair also makes sure that regular committee meetings start in earnest after the New Year holiday. In January and February, the committee meets biweekly, and in March

they meet weekly to ensure coordination. As the event has grown, a greater need for planning and coordination has become apparent, and the continuing ability to produce the event on a completely volunteer basis is now questionable.

>> One of the group's fundamental beliefs from the beginning has been to work in partnership with the city. They get an official parade permit every year from Detroit City Council, and work with the health department to allow the festival to offer food and beer. They also procure fire effects permits from the fire department. Every year the Detroit Police Department helps with public safety. For the last two years, they have closed the entire route to vehicle traffic.

>> The strongest partner to date has been Midtown Detroit, Inc., a local nonprofit planning and development organization that supports the physical maintenance and revitalization of the Midtown Detroit neighborhood, while working to enhance public awareness, appreciation, and use of the district. Midtown Detroit, Inc. has supported the event financially since the second year.

>> They have also partnered with both Midtown Detroit, Inc. and Cityscape Detroit, another nonprofit, to act as fiduciaries for the event. In 2014, they received a generous grant from the Knight Foundation.

>> Another of the organizers' fundamental beliefs is to engage and celebrate the small businesses along the route and throughout the city. A portion of the Marche's costs are covered by small businesses and individuals who see the Marche as a positive boon to the neighborhood and Detroit in general.

SOCIOECONOMIC IMPACT

>> As an intrinsic aspect of the event, the district's assets, public spaces, small businesses, shops, restaurants, and bars are also featured as a way of further building community. Many local businesses host events and have special offers during that week, from offering exclusive themed tee shirt designs, to food and drink specials in honor of the Marche, such as the "El Diablito" pizza, the "Sangre Del Nain" drink, Creole beans and rice, and an annual crawfish boil.

>> In its grant application to the Knight Foundation, the Marche du Nain Rouge committee offered this as part of its stated purpose and impact: "Bringing people together for the Marche, and having them move through a neighborhood bolsters not just street life, but also the local economy in significant ways. During a few hours on an otherwise quiet Sunday afternoon, upwards of $50,000 is spent at more than two dozen local establishments along the route, as parade-goers patronize bars, shops, and restaurants. In the past few years, sponsorship has also grown beyond the Cass Corridor neighborhood to adjacent area establishments that view the Marche as a way to grow business, awareness, and authentic community identity."

>> Since the beginning, the Marche has been a family-friendly event celebrating Detroit's diversity and rich cultural heritage, helping to reinforce the city's growing sense of community pride.

>> "Like similar events encouraging people to experience a neighborhood or city, the Marche du Nain Rouge creates a positive sense of place in Detroit, by connecting people through art and the city's history

to an historic neighborhood, the Cass Corridor," said committee member Francis Grunow.

LESSONS LEARNED

>> Don't let "no" stop you from doing something. Just because there is no precedent doesn't mean it can't be done. That being said, if the event is to be done on a repeated basis, getting official buy-in early is important. Working with the city as a partner is vital to the longevity of the Marche. There have been hiccups and compromise along the way, but the overall goal of producing a positive event to benefit the city has allowed the Marche to continue.

>> While leadership is vital to a project's success, it is just as important to understand what a committee is capable of and committed to early on in the process. If there is not a shared sense of commitment to an outcome, then there's a problem.

>> Figure out how to make a project or event fit into modules so that if not enough volunteer effort or resources are procured, the event can be scaled appropriately. Conversely, if the event can grow over the years, figuring out which elements can be built up in the future can help with sustainability.

>> Partner with a nonprofit to allow funders and supporters to make tax-deductible donations. However, expectations between entities should be made crystal clear from the outset, ideally in the form of a memorandum of understanding, or something similar.

>> Understand your audience, but also allow them to help shape the event. One of the more interesting aspects of the Marche is that the parade is the audience. It is a fun way of getting maximum amount of creativity with a relatively modest amount of investment.

(ENDNOTES)

1 "Detroit," Wikipedia, accessed April 23, 2014, http://en.wikipedia.org/wiki/Detroit.

2 "History of the Nain Rouge," Marche du Nain Rouge, accessed April 24, 2014, http://marchedunainrouge.com/history/.

3 "Tour de Troit," Tour de Troit, accessed June 18, 2014, http://www.tour-de-troit.org.

4 Ashley Woods, "Nain Rouge 2013: Pure Detroit Captures The Marche Through Detroit's Cass Corridor (VIDEO)," The Huffington Post, March 25, 2013, http://www.huffingtonpost.com/2013/03/25/nain-rouge-2013-detroit-video_n_2949080.html.

Moving Placemaking Forward Through
Special Events

- The Michigan Festivals and Events Association (MFEA) is a statewide nonprofit organization serving communities, events, festivals, fairs, businesses, and volunteers throughout Michigan. They promote local events, festivals, and destinations, and provide technical assistance, training, and education to members. MFEA marketing efforts to promote members include a statewide distributed brochure listing Festival & Event Members by month, an e-version Membership Directory, and Buyers' Guide featuring MFEA Vendors that is given to all members. Their website at www.michiganfun.com lists all members by category and is available to the public.[1]

- The International Festivals Association provides worldwide resources for festival and event planners with global affiliates including IFEA North America.[2]

- The International Town-Gown Association provides a network of resources to assist civic leaders, university officials, faculty, residents, and students to collaborate on common services, programs, academic research, and citizen issues, creating an improved quality of life for all.[3]

(ENDNOTES)

1 Michigan Festivals and Events Association, accessed June 12, 2014, http://mfea.org.

2 "About Us," International Festivals and Events Association, accessed June 12, 2014, http://www.ifea.com/joomla2_5/index.php/joomla-overview.

3 "Mission And Vision," International Town Gown Association, accessed June 12, 2014, http://itgau.org/content.aspx?ContentID=1438.

Water. It's as elemental as earth, wind, and fire. No civilization has ever been founded where water did not exist. It has helped spread mankind across the planet, provided sustenance, a source of energy, and formed natural and protective borders for societies.

Indeed, nearly every modern city was founded on a waterway, which provided a route for moving trade goods in and out, a cheap source of power for industry, and unfortunately, a vessel for dumping waste. In fact, it's only been in relatively recent times that the urban waterfront has come to be valued mainly as an aesthetic or recreational asset.

Today, cities around the globe are casting a fresh eye on their historic waterfronts, and reclaiming them as core elements for creating an authentic sense of place.

Project for Public Spaces has identified 10 qualities of a great waterfront destination:[1]

1. Surrounding buildings that enhance the public space

2. Limits on residential development

3. Year-round and around-the-clock activities

4. Flexible design that fosters adaptability

5. Creative amenities that boost everyone's enjoyment

6. Easy access by boat, bike, and foot

7. Local identity is showcased

8. The water itself draws attention

9. Iconic buildings that serve a variety of functions

10. Good management that maintains the community vision

WATERFRONTS

Restoring an environmentally damaged and highly industrialized waterfront can be a monumental undertaking that requires significant funding, expert design and engineering, and years of planning and development. But when done correctly, the rewards can go far beyond all the time and money spent, to reorient the city's identity toward its greatest public space.

(ENDNOTES)

1 "10 Qualities of a Great Waterfront Destination," Project for Public Spaces, accessed March 14, 2014, http://www.pps.org/reference/10_qualities_of_a_great_waterfront/.

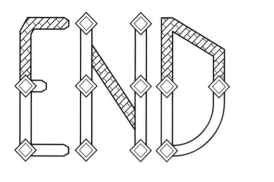

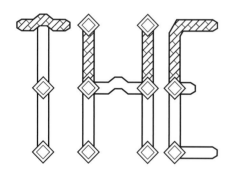
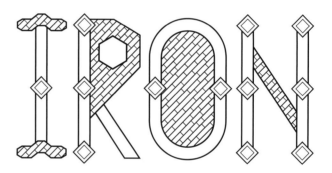
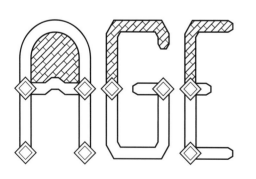

END OF THE IRON AGE

Reinventing an
Industrial Harbor as a
Waterfront Destination

For more than a century, the icy winds of Lake Superior had blown swirling clouds of black and red dust across the docks and railroad tracks crammed along the great northern bay of Marquette. No one standing on the crowded, noisy waterfront had any doubts that iron ore was the lifeblood pumping through the heart of Marquette. Since the mid-1800s, its vast and booming industrial network had linked the mines of northern Michigan's remote Upper Peninsula (U.P.) to the iron-hungry world beyond Lake Superior's frigid shores. A ceaseless stream of rail cars rocked and roared along an overhead train trestle running straight through the center of town to a massive ore dock at the Lower Harbor. A rust-colored fog billowed from the chutes pouring iron pellets into the holds of freighters bound for Chicago and other ports in the lower Great Lakes. Huge mountains of coal blocked the shoreline view, waiting to feed the furnaces of a massive power plant standing on the city's eastern edge. The smell of diesel oil stung your nostrils, and the mineral dust stained the snow, streets, and buildings alike, as if some giant child had smudged dirty fingers across the city's surface.

It was the peak of the industrial age. Wealth born of iron and lumber had built a city unsurpassed in its time, almost anywhere else in the country this far north. Even after an 1868 fire devastated the central business district, destroying more than 100 wooden structures in its path, the downtown was rebuilt with a fast and stubborn vengeance. In fact, the city's only concession to the disaster was a resolution passed by the city commission decreeing that from that point forward, anything in town had to be built of stone. In response, new churches and government buildings reared up as grand monuments of classical architecture carved in native brownstone. Bigger and grander than ever, downtown Marquette thrived as the cultural and economic center for the scattered, remote population of the entire U.P.

But all along the bay-front streets, every building had its back turned to the waterfront that had bankrolled its existence. Like most port cities of the time, the harbor wasn't a place for tourism or recreation, and water wasn't valued as a resource in itself. The bay was simply an industrial and commercial reality to be tolerated and ignored, a necessary but unsightly mess of pollution, noise, mechanical hazards, and toxic waste. It was a reality that couldn't last forever.

Meanwhile, the world was changing. By 1971, the Lower Harbor had ceased industrial shipping operations, with the freighter traffic shifted to the Upper Harbor west of town. Even at nearly 1,000 feet long and 85 feet high, a mere 40 years after its construction in 1931, the ore dock was already too small to handle the newer, larger freighters plying the lakes. Gloomy economic times were echoing throughout the state, and commerce slowed on the Great Lakes shipping routes.

But the harbor's industrial brownfield remained, a black eye on the urban face of a city struggling to reimagine itself in a quieter and less prosperous post-industrial era.

Like many adults who grew up in Marquette in the decades between the 1960s and 1980s, current City Manager William Vajda remembers a waterfront that was anything but scenic.

"This was a place where your mom didn't want you to be. The port was home to longshoremen and railroad workers, big trucks, cranes, trains, and hookers and hobos," said Vajda. "And if you did go down there, Mom would find out quick, because all the stuff you were playing in was stuck to you. You'd go home covered with creosote and coal dust and diesel oil, and there was no way you could lie your way out of where you'd been."

Pat Black, executive director of the Marquette County Convention and Visitors Bureau, vividly recalls scores of homeless men living in tents and makeshift junk and cardboard shelters, clustered along a wooded drainage seep beneath the shadow of the railroad trestle.

"They called it Bum's Jungle, and that was someplace nobody was supposed to go. The girls never went, of course, but some of the teenage boys would go down to get one of the 'uncles' to buy their beer," said Black. "During the day they'd go begging door to door, and the women would feed them lunches. In the winter they'd vanish, I don't know where, but when spring came, there they'd be again, like they'd never left."

By the end of the 1980s, Marquette's Lower Harbor had clearly outlived any remaining usefulness as a commercial shipping port. Once-crowded warehouses sat abandoned, roofs rotting and floorboards crumbling. Pilings from storm-wrecked docks stood decaying in the bay. Unused rail tracks and trestles rusted in place like industrial skeletons. Some cities might have simply given up, fading into grey ghosts of their former glory days. Not Marquette. If mining and shipping could no longer support the city, they would find something else that would. But first, the city itself would have to become something else in order to attract that new economy.

It was time for a change.

"There are still a lot of places in 'coal country' where this kind of heavy industry and company town mentality is still strong, and they end up looking a lot like towns around here. When Marquette abandoned mining as their principal business decades ago, it proved to be the best decision that could have possibly been made," said Vajda. "It forced diversification to other business clusters, to get other things going, and now you can see the result."

"When you look at Marquette now, it's very easy to illustrate what placemaking is all about. There's a very stark contrast between communities based on what they want to be, and what kind of place they want to make for themselves."

SETTING A COURSE FOR CHANGE

While the speed of change over the past decade has been highly visible and dramatic, much of the groundwork was laid much earlier by forward-thinking civic leaders. About 1980, the city had formed a Downtown Development Authority (DDA) in response to DDA legislation passed the year before. Its twofold goals were to revitalize the downtown and reclaim the waterfront as a city asset. A community vision had also begun to form at that time, of transforming the underused waterfront into a tourism area built on the region's rich cultural history and abundant natural beauty and recreational resources.

Marquette was also blessed with two key assets that were essential to its transformation from industrial hub to a regional center of tourism and culture:

Northern Michigan University and Marquette General Hospital. Besides providing many of the resources and facilities of a knowledge-based economy, they offered a ready-made human resource of highly educated professionals and ambitious, enthusiastic young people. When tapped by the city to serve on boards and commissions and empowered with a key role in reshaping their city, they rose to the challenge. By intentionally seeking input from the community at large, the city was able to develop a 20-year master plan that reached beyond the whims and will of any particular council of elected officials. The plan was a product that belonged to the entire community.

That sense of public ownership enabled the city to move quickly and efficiently on the path to transformation, even amid the usual range of personal and political frictions found in any unit of government. Implementation was aggressive, and because the plan had such clearly defined goals, the city manager and staff were able to swiftly identify and seize upon opportunities, reordering priorities as needed. Citizens offered support instead of blockades, and because of that, they were able to see rapid, steady progress which further fueled their ongoing enthusiasm and support. Public confidence in the vision grew, civic engagement increased, pride swelled, and the city found itself exponentially richer in social capital—a highly prized, but often elusive commodity.

The first and most visible change was the clean-up of the cinder pond, an industrial waste site once used as a coal unloading facility adjacent to the first ore dock and furnace, where in the late 1800s slag was dumped into the water along with sawdust from a shingle mill. Since the old coal yard was no longer needed, owner G.N. Spear had offered it to the city in his will on the

condition it be used for recreational purposes. The city purchased the parcel in 1977 for $300,000 using a mix of federal funds, matching local dollars, and philanthropic support from the Shiras Institute. The green space was finished in 1981, and local banker Ellwood Mattson then spearheaded efforts to raise the final $500,000 needed to complete the park.[1]

At the time the property was purchased, some residents had scoffed at the idea. Who would use a park there? But it didn't take long for the naysayers to become true believers too.

Located just north of the ore dock in Marquette's Lower Harbor, the 22-acre Mattson Lower Harbor Park was dedicated/named the "Ellwood A. Mattson Park" during the June 26, 1989 City Commission meeting. (The "Lower Harbor Park" site had been open to the public since 1981, but subject to ongoing remediation and improvement. During those years, many non-profit groups had contributed park improvements which were coordinated with the city and approved by the City Commission, with financial support from the city and state via a variety of grants.) The grassy open space area offers park benches, picnic tables, a period-style concession and restroom facility, a boat ramp and nearby breakwater, and a children's playground with a large wooden play-scape built with community donations and volunteer labor. The shoreline bike path runs through the park and an illuminated walkway with period style lighting parallels the waterfront along the bulkhead. Fishermen flock to the park in the spring and fall for coho and chinook salmon as well as rainbow, lake, and brown trout.

In just a few years, the park has become the city's most popular location for special events, playing host to such activities as the Seafood Festival, the

International Food Festival, Winterfest, and an ongoing schedule of concerts, fireworks, and other large gatherings. A lighted outdoor ice rink is located in the park during the winter months. The 101-slip Cinder Pond Marina, completed in 1995, is located immediately east of the park.

"Once they started doing their festivals down there, it's been so successful everywhere down here," said Black. "There's probably something going on every weekend. The first year of Beer Fest, I thought it was going to just be a local thing. They had under 1,000 people. The second year they went up. This year they sold out in presales and had 3,500 show up, and it was raining."

In fact, the only problem might be too much success.

"Part of the challenge now is that this has become such a core place on the waterfront for so many big prestigious events, and we're getting so many more tourists, that the infrastructure demands are having an impact," said Vajda. "In the last three to five years, some residents in the immediate area are getting event fatigue! But their real estate values have skyrocketed too in a period of maybe 10 years."

Still, event planners must deal with early curfews to avoid becoming a public nuisance, and there is talk about developing alternative venues nearby that would be less disruptive to residents, Black said.

Immediately to the west of the park on Front Street, another keystone event occurred in the city's rebirth: the grand re-opening of Marquette's former crown jewel, the Northland Hotel, as the completely renovated and refurbished Landmark Inn.

When it opened in 1930, the historic Northland Hotel was the tallest building in the entire Upper Peninsula, playing host to such luminaries as Amelia Earhart, Abbot and Costello, Duke Ellington, and Louis Armstrong. But by the 1970s, its social dominance had waned along with the city's economic fortunes. Following years of slow decay, the doors were finally closed for good in 1982, and its elegant furnishings and fixtures auctioned off.

Encouraged by the positive changes occurring in Marquette, local entrepreneurs Christine and Bruce Pesola purchased the structure in 1995, and set about restoring the hotel to its former glory, even salvaging the original marble staircase and brass hand railings and using the original architectural plans to faithfully restore its décor.

"It was really an eyesore when they bought it. The windows were out and there were literally doves and pigeons flying in and out," said Black. "At first they didn't know quite what they were going to do with it, maybe open a Super 8 or something. But Christine is a lover of antiques, so they went that historic route instead."

"When they opened the doors the first day, she started crying because she didn't know what to do and they had guests coming in. The hotel rates were the highest anybody had ever seen in Marquette, and everybody said 'you'll never do it'. But she has done it. It was an instant success."

History and architecture buffs have made it a favorite spot on the circuit of national historic hotels. Business travelers connected with the university and hospital are also frequent guests, while a steady flow of casual tourists are drawn to its elegant ambiance and convenient location in the heart of downtown.

The park and hotel proved to be perfect catalysts of change. As the domino effect continued to spread and the DDA's downtown revitalization efforts increased, vacancies began to fill all across the central business district.

Development of the park property also turned out to be the perfect catalyst to revitalize the nearby bay-view area into a new mixed-use residential neighborhood. Just a few short years after the marina was completed, the city's first waterfront condominiums were built across the street from the park. When they were built in 2004, Harbor Ridge Townhomes and Condominiums—affectionately nicknamed "The Birdhouses" by residents—sold at $330,000-$400,000 per unit. In less than 10 years, those price tags had risen to more than $500,000, according to Community Services Director Karl Zueger.

In turn, that success spurred investors' interest in the empty, deteriorating warehouses and rail shops along the entire downtown waterfront on now-scenic Lakeshore Drive.

Soon afterward, the nearby Flanigan Brothers building—a moving and storage warehouse built in 1927—was reconstructed into a mixed-use development of office space and six condominiums that currently sell for about $425,000. With many of the building's architectural features maintained, it serves as a perfect example of how historic reuse can enhance a community's identity and sense of place.

The people buying the new waterfront condominiums include affluent empty nesters downsizing from their former suburban homes into walkable downtown apartments and condominiums, and young adults seeking a more vibrant urban lifestyle.

"There's a pretty big difference in expectations between someone who's 48 and someone who's 78, but by and large we're getting people who want to be part of an active downtown," said Vajda. "We're even getting some young professional athletes who were originally from northern Michigan who come back and buy apartments here."

The change has been profound for Vajda, who himself had moved away to go to school and was gone for 30 years before returning to his hometown in 2010.

"My most amazing impression was that all the things I really love about Marquette are still here and have only gotten better, while things that weren't so great diminished," said Vajda. "You can see the skyline and character of the harbor has become substantially different within the last 100 years, from an area that was heavy industrial to one now dedicated primarily to placemaking. A lot of the industrial character has been eliminated, and just one street over the retail, wholesale, and residential character has been preserved."

Perhaps nothing illustrates that socioeconomic shift more than the re-orientation of the buildings themselves.

"In the past, everything was facing away from the lake. The last place people wanted to focus their attention was this horrid industrial, nasty area," Vajda said. "Now, 30 years later, everything is facing 180 degrees the opposite way. The buildings now face the most valuable asset that we have, which is Lake Superior and that beautiful coastal view. For me, that is the best insight into what's happened in Marquette that has completely changed the character of the town. You couldn't have a more profound change of direction."

FORM AND FUNCTION:
BUILDING BLOCKS FOR PLACE

A fundamental reason for this success is something that is mostly invisible and incomprehensible to the general public, and undoubtedly sounds like "inside baseball" jargon to those outside the planning and zoning world: the city's adoption of form-based codes to expedite redevelopment and occupancy of unused buildings.

What this means, in essence, is tossing out the decades-old zoning philosophy that helped create urban sprawl, and replacing it with an approach that encourages high-quality, mixed-use development.

According to the Form-Based Codes Institute, this alternative approach to traditional zoning "fosters predictable built results and a high-quality public realm by using physical form (rather than separation of uses) as the organizing principle for the code. They are regulations, not mere guidelines, adopted into city or county law. Form-based codes offer a powerful alternative to conventional zoning."[2]

"Traditional" zoning codes typically require developers to adhere to minimum lot sizes and building setbacks, onsite parking requirements, street width standards designed for car flow, and the restriction of uses into separate zones. Rather than achieving their intended goal of a high standard for development, all these rules instead work together to create single-use development spread out over large areas, with an emphasis on ease of use for cars rather than people.

"Form-based codes address the relationship between building façades and the public realm, the form and mass of buildings in relation to one another, and the scale and types of streets and blocks. The regulations and standards in form-based codes are presented in both words and clearly drawn diagrams and other visuals. They are keyed to a regulating plan that designates the appropriate form and scale (and therefore, character) of development, rather than only distinctions in land-use types."

"This approach contrasts with conventional zoning's focus on the micromanagement and segregation of land uses, and the control of development intensity through abstract and uncoordinated parameters (e.g.,... dwellings per acre, setbacks, parking ratios...), to the neglect of an integrated built form. Not to be confused with design guidelines or general statements of policy, form-based codes are regulatory, not advisory. They are drafted to implement a community plan. They try to achieve a community vision based on time-tested forms of urbanism. Ultimately, a form-based code is a tool; the quality of development outcomes depends on the quality and objectives of the community plan that a code implements."[3]

It's a philosophical approach to zoning that has resulted in a vibrant downtown redevelopment vision focused on mixed-use new and historic buildings offering condominiums, townhomes, restaurants, and commercial retail and office space. Several large warehouse buildings and large tracts of land nearby were also developed into apartment buildings. All of the residences abut to a citywide trail system that links the waterfront's linear park with many regional amenities.

"Form-based code has helped to preserve the character and integrity of the lower harbor and downtown architectural culture," said Community Development Director Dennis Stachewicz. "The code provides a clear guideline for developers wishing to invest in the district. It also helps to protect their investment by ensuring other developments will be accountable for the same requirements and design quality. It also ensures the public that the area's look and sense of place will be preserved, while development continues to evolve."

In Marquette, that look and sense of place is unmistakable, from the majestic courthouse featured in the 1959 Jimmy Stewart film "Anatomy of a Murder," to the iconic Bunny Bread logo on the window of the Upper Peninsula Children's Museum, salvaged from the city's beloved former wholesale bread factory.

"All these buildings are made with the same Jacobsville sandstone quarried just two miles up the road. You can't build more local than that!" Vajda said. "These inter-generational legacies really tie in with our sense of place. When you visit a historic building here, there's a good chance you'll run into somebody whose grandfather helped build it, or their grandmother might have worked in it. That's why they're so well and lovingly preserved. Those memories still live in their stones."

"A big part of our local preservation efforts use the legacy of our past as a basis for our vision moving forward. We want to preserve our history so we can enjoy and honor it by using it."

BEYOND THE WATERFRONT

Meanwhile, serendipity was working to the city's advantage at the harbor's eastern end, at the site of the old Bum's Jungle.

Wisconsin Central Ltd. Railroad was negotiating the sale of its company to Canadian National Railroad. But Wisconsin Central still owned the 29-acre parcel of contaminated property. Seizing on the opportunity, the city launched into negotiations with Wisconsin Central in an effort to obtain the property before the company's sale to Canadian National, both for its development potential and to increase public access to the waterfront.

As luck would have it, the State of Michigan was unrolling its Clean Michigan Initiative Grant (CMI)[4] program at the same time. The city applied for a CMI grant for the brownfield cleanup and acquired the property in 2001. With that financial support from the State of Michigan, the city was able to invest over $11 million in demolition, environmental remediation, and public infrastructure to reclaim the site as a viable green space ripe for redevelopment.

During the clean-up, a creek that was previously funneled into culverts was reopened and now gurgles through the property as a natural waterway crossed by two scenic bridges—one for trail users and one for vehicles. They are symbolic of how this city has focused on building for people, and not just for cars. The newly renamed Founders Landing is a nod to its heritage as the first landing site of settlers to the area. A re-enactment of the landing is now an annual city tradition.

It's important to note that the city designated all of the property's lakeshore as public green space, with mixed-use development plans for the area between the green space and the highway. The first condominium units are constructed and occupied, with immediate front door access to public green space, walking and cycling trails, and waterfront views, with easy walkability to downtown businesses and the Lower Harbor's many recreational opportunities and events. A hotel is also on the site with remaining space slated for more residential and mixed-use development.

In addition to Harbor Ridge Townhome Condominiums and the Flannigan Building, there have been several large and small private residential and commercial development projects that have occurred since the city made its public waterfront investment. They include LS&I condo/commercial property, Berube Condominium property, Elizabeth's Chop House, the Rosewood Building, and at least two private residential reuse projects that are located on Lakeshore Blvd. Total investment conservatively would total over $30 million.

It's an economic development boom unequaled since the city's industrial heyday, and one that has impacted the entire city in a profoundly positive way.

Stachewicz said that the Downtown Development District alone has experienced private investment of more than $60 million over the last decade. Once fully realized, private investment in Founders Landing will total over $40 million.

Until recently, one of the biggest remnants of the past still towered above Front Street: the overhead train trestle connected to the Lower Harbor ore dock. Unsightly as it was, the trestle proved to be one of the city's most controversial items, with many people strongly in favor of keeping the trestle intact.

"Our commercial freight yard was here on the water, and in the old days it would run right through the middle of the intersection, and head out of town to the

Today, the city
of Marquette
essentially owns
and controls its
entire waterfront,
a fact that has
had a profound
impact on its
sense of place as a
scenic waterfront
community.

west," Vajda said.

The trestle was eventually removed, opening up a beautiful skyline and scenic vista upon entering the downtown. Loyal to the city's heritage, the city hired a local artist to make benches from the metal remnants of the trestle. No two are alike. These delightful, iconic benches are dotting the city's Rosewood Walkway, where former on-ground rails used to be, leading from the lower harbor area to the back of the downtown. The city then strategically began working with businesses to open the backs of their buildings to this area, essentially linking this Rosewood Walkway to area businesses downtown. The Walkway has been a smashing success as a link from the lower harbor to downtown businesses. Marquette Commons was also built in this area. It is the site of a three-season farmers market, winter ice skating and other year-round events, often in conjunction with events at the lower harbor.

"This is another way we've recaptured some of that space," said Vajda. "Rather than just filling it with something, we've turned it into an area where people like to spend time."

HIKES, BIKES, BOATS, AND BREW

The other essential element in Marquette's placemaking plan is its focus on tourism and recreation as industries with tremendous growth potential. The key has been building on the region's existing assets while exploring new opportunities.

Today, the city of Marquette essentially owns and controls its entire waterfront, a fact that has had a profound impact on its sense of place as a scenic waterfront community.

"Unlike most cities, you won't see any development directly on the water. It's all publicly accessible. You can feel confident if you're walking anywhere in Marquette along the beach, you're doing it on public property. That's been a core philosophy of this city since it was founded, and it's never been challenged," said Vajda.

Black said that the Lake Superior waterfront is still the city's biggest asset.

"If there's a freighter coming, there could be 50 or 60 people waiting because it's so fascinating. We, who live here, take it for granted, but there's no other place you can get up closer to an ore freighter. There are a lot of places along Lake Michigan where you can't even get a view of the water. Here, it's available to people, and that's huge. I think that's why our tourism has a lot to do with the lake. It just has a different feel than any other place."

Marquette's unique sense of place might start at the waterfront, but it extends in all directions, thanks in large part to a growing network of recreational trails.

Marquette's mountain biking trails have been in existence for at least 20 years, with new trails constantly being built. Currently, more than 25 miles of single-track exist in the Noquemanon Trail Network (NTN) just south of Marquette. The single-track system has earned national acclaim as a premier mountain biking destination from Bike Magazine, Silent Sports Magazine, and others. Efforts are currently underway to gain the coveted "Epic Trail" designation from the International Mountain Biking Association.

In the winter, snow biking is coming on strong as the latest recreational trend to hit the region, and Marquette is taking full advantage of it. The specially built bikes feature extremely wide, heavy-treaded tires; hence the nickname "fat tire biking."

"The new winter market for us is definitely the snow bikes. For the last several years we just haven't had the snow we used to up here; it's narrowed down really to a few good weeks in February. So as the snowmobile group has narrowed down, we've looked to the snow bikers as the hot new thing," said Black. "They now groom the south trails for them and it's huge. At some point, it will get too crowded and it'll ruin the experience, so now they're looking into it on the mountain biking trails on the west end of the county."

In addition to the NTN, the city and its neighbors are developing an extensive multi-use trail network connecting the entire outlying region and key points within each community, such as Presque Isle Park, which is itself a major tourist draw.

When completed, the Iron Ore Heritage Trail will be a 48-mile, multi-use, year-round trail from Republic Township to Kawbawgam Road in Chocolay Township. Signage along the surfaced trail will connect people to historic sites relating the story of more than 150 years of mining in the Marquette Iron Range. The surfaced trail is being developed for a multitude of uses. When possible, parallel but separate trail sections are being designed for motorized uses such as snowmobiles and ATVs.

"They produced 10,000 maps in July, and they were all gone by September. It's not unusual to see 500-600 people a day using that trail network," Black said. "I love riding it out to Negaunee where you can get out and walk through the Lost City, where they moved a whole neighborhood out when they started having cave-ins from all the underground mining. It's spooky, with stairs that go to nowhere, and little markers where the houses used to be. That's a real part of our history here."

The multi-use trails are expanding beyond the region's popularity as a mountain biking destination, to encompass recreational bike touring and bike commuting.

"We don't want to just focus on mountain biking because we don't want to become just one kind of biking destination," said Black. "Our bike trails are really family friendly. You can park your car out at the Welcome Center in Harvey, ride along the shoreline of Marquette Bay, then come through town and bike around Presque Isle Park. The ore boats that come in and load iron ore pellets out of Presque Isle are a huge attraction."

The biking culture has helped spark a surge of new businesses around the city.

"Brew pubs have just gone nuts and it all ties back into the biking thing. Right now, we've got three or four new ones and another opening up," said Black. "We've got one brew pub that opens at 4 p.m. and they usually close by 9 p.m. because they run out of beer. Now, with the snow bikers, we'll drive by in a blizzard and see they are sitting on the porch drinking a beer."

Some of the new brew pubs are embracing the creative spirit of entrepreneurism by allowing patrons to bring in their own food, thereby avoiding the cost and complexity of food service. Ordering a pizza delivered to your table at a pub has become a favorite pastime among locals, especially the college crowd. Vajda said that the reverse could also happen if the state's liquor code is changed to allow a "bring your own bottle" option for restaurants without beer and wine licenses.

That free spirit and sense of adventure has become part of the flavor in Marquette's sense of place.

"Having the college kids here helps too. They give us instant cool. Nowadays, you see visitors coming here and they've all got kayaks on top of their car and bikes on the back. We're not just a recreation community, but we've kind of developed into that," said

Black. "All of it is available to the public, that's the big thing. The people of Marquette come down and enjoy it too, not just the visitors. There's so much that's available everywhere."

FACING FORWARD

In June 2013, the Veridea Group announced a new development called Liberty Way at the intersection of Washington and Lincoln streets. The three-phase development includes a 28,406-square-foot office building completed in 2013 to house mBank, Veridea Group offices, and Illinois-based Myefski Architects.

The second phase is scheduled for completion in 2014. The $30 million investment will offer a new Staybridge Suites upscale hotel; a 170-stall heated underground parking garage with electric car recharging stations; and a bicycle repair and maintenance facility just off the path of the existing trail[5] where Liberty Way will connect to the city bike path behind it. All told, it will include more than 130,000-square-feet of mixed-use space, including commercial and retail, and add more than 100 jobs to the community. Backers include the Marquette Brownfield Redevelopment Authority.

But even amid the surge of new economic development, Marquette hasn't lost sight of the history that fueled its founding, and still serves as the core of its authentic sense of identity. Like a silent, rusting iron giant standing up to its knees in the bay, the massive ore dock still overlooks the city's waterfront, just as it has for more than 80 years. It is a constant and faithful reminder of the city's past, and a spiritual sentinel for the future.

"It's become iconic. This old ore dock is the last of its kind on Lake Superior, and originally they preserved it for nostalgic, sentimental reasons. But as it turns out, it was a good thing for practical reasons too," said Vajda.

"They've since realized it's a huge windbreak, and if you took that down you wouldn't have the sheltered harbor behind it. Nobody actually thought about that at the time, but it turns out that was probably the most valuable reason for keeping it up."

In late 2013, the city council approved spending funds on a structural analysis to explore potential public uses beyond the current allowed use as a dock or promenade. Ambitious architects have proposed design ideas featuring unique condominium units and even possibly a restaurant within its structure.

But the city's new face hasn't turned a blind eye on its remaining lake industries. If anything, it has helped those long-standing businesses continue to thrive.

"We still have a working waterfront. You can see the state research vessel for the fisheries, we have some charter businesses, a tour boat, and the city's official tall ship. We actually have three different fishing industries that work out of the harbor. We have two tribal fisheries and the last commercial fishery in Michigan on Lake Superior, so it's still an active business," Vajda said.

One of the historic downtown businesses tied to the working waterfront is the Vierling Saloon, which has stood at the corner of South Front and Main streets for more than 100 years.

"They actually still walk down to the harbor each day and get the fish fresh off the dock, and they cook it later that morning, so you can't get a fresher meal unless you're cooking it on the boat," said Vajda.

Another cherished remnant of the past is an old stone abutment that still sits at the base of the former train trestle, now transformed into one of the city's many small pocket parks.

"We've got all kinds of these former industrial areas where we're trying to keep a balance between redevelopment and green space," said Vajda. "People here take a dim view of overbuilding."

Marquette's rebirth also reflects a better understanding of regional economics and its place as the metropolitan center of the Upper Peninsula.

"If you drew a one-hour commuting bubble around Marquette, you're no longer discussing a community of 20,000 or 70,000, depending how many students are around town on any given day; you're actually the center of a community of 220,000 people. Once that was really understood, the community started to figure out they're creating opportunities for a different consumer base, and that attracted a different kind of developer," said Vajda. "What we're seeing now are old Marquette businesses becoming more innovative, and new entrepreneurs with bold ideas who are creating new opportunities. So we're getting a mix of a lot of different things going on. Does that require unique people? Probably."

Today's Marquette is still a work in progress. But by anyone's measure, the placemaking vision launched two decades ago is now much more reality than dream. The waterfront makeover has indeed become a tide that is lifting all boats.

"Once the views of the community change, it's amazing how fast the physical environment can change. Grass doesn't grow on a good idea in Marquette. As soon as inspiration takes hold, somebody always acts and tries to make a go of it," Vajda said. "We're trying to make government as responsive and flexible as possible to keep up with the spirit of the community. Sometimes that's our biggest challenge. Our residents want to move so quickly, it takes us a while to make sure we do so in a balanced way."

(ENDNOTES)

1 "Touring Marquette," Avery Color Studios, Inc., 2004.

2 "What Are form-Based Codes?, Form-Based Codes Institute, accessed November 25, 2013, http://formbasedcodes.org/definition.

3 Ibid.

4 "Clean Michigan Initiative (CMI) Overview," Department of Environmental Quality, accessed June 18, 2014, http://www.michigan.gov/deq/0,1607,7-135-3307_31116---,00.html.

5 "Veridea Announces Liberty Way Development in Marquette," Upper Peninsula's Second Wave, June 5, 2013, accessed December 17, 2013, http://up.secondwavemedia.com/devnews/verideaconstructionmqt6513.aspx.

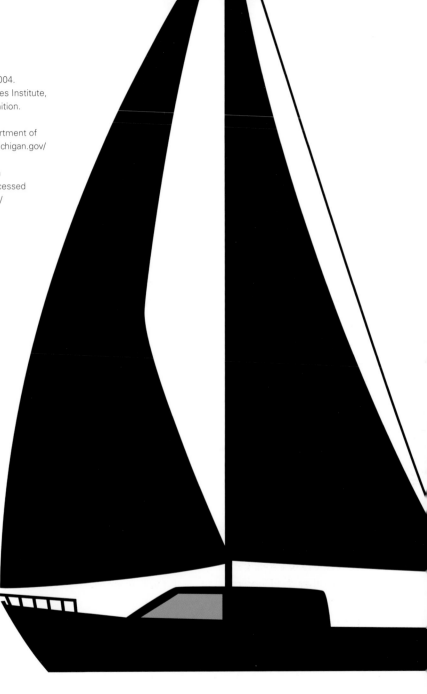

CASE STUDY

Silver Beach Center

St. Joseph, Michigan — Pop. 8,365

PROJECT SCOPE

Imagine you're at the end of a hard work week at your office in downtown Chicago. Your bags are already packed so you head straight to Union Station and hop the train for a leisurely ride up the far side coast of Lake Michigan. Just a few hours later, you're stepping onto the platform at St. Joseph, suddenly immersed in another world full of sun, sand, and clear blue water. The gaily painted Victorian-style depot is hopping with people sipping craft beer and scooping up thick slabs of hot pizza, laughing and chatting as they gaze out toward the water along the open-air windows of the Silver Beach Pizza parlor. Beyond them, the white sand beach spreads out to meet the rolling blue waves of Lake Michigan. Children squeal with laughter as they run through a series of water fountains shooting up toward the sky, the sunlight forming rainbows in the spray. Beyond it lies the carousel. Above it all, couples linger on a network of stairways and decks that climb the steep sand bluff to the bustling shops and eateries of a picture book downtown.

Welcome to St. Joseph, reimagined and revitalized as a place where people once again come to play, party, and watch the colors of a perfect Lake Michigan sunset.

Sitting on the southeastern shore of Lake Michigan about 90 miles out of Chicago, St. Joseph was long a favorite haunt for Chicago tourists seeking a picturesque lakefront holiday within easy car and rail distance from the bustle of big city life. Quaint cottages sprung up along the white sand beaches, and in 1891, the Silver Beach Amusement Park opened on the shorefront land below the bluff between the lake and the mouth of the St. Joseph River. The park offered a variety of concessions, games, carnival rides, and other attractions, including a roller coaster, carousel, and the famous Shadowland Ballroom.

By the 1920s, the local economy was also booming with an influx of industry surrounding a hugely successful washing machine manufacturing business that would eventually become the Whirlpool Corporation in 1948. For nearly a century, St. Joseph enjoyed a cozy spot nestled in the heart of the "Riviera of the Midwest," reaping the rewards of a prosperous economy and scenic locale.

But all that had changed by the late 1960s and 1970s. The park buildings decayed as maintenance and repair costs soared. Crime rose in the park and the crowds started to stay away. Finally, the Silver Beach Amusement Park was shut down for good in 1971. Vacant property and antiquated industrial sites blemished the once-pristine lakefront. By 2004, the city's downtown was visibly struggling too. As local shoppers turned away from the traditional downtown to the new big box stores and malls in the outlying townships, the vacancy rate hovered at 33 percent in downtown retail buildings.

But civic and business leaders had a vision that the city's future prosperity lay in reclaiming its once-magnificent waterfront, which would also help to bring visitors and residents alike back to its neglected downtown. They teamed up to create an ongoing program of outdoor public art exhibits and special activities to increase foot traffic downtown and to help recreate the city's sense of place as a scenic tourist destination.

It was only natural that the first art project harkened back to the old Silver Beach glory days. In 1997, the Silver Beach Carousel Society had been formed to purchase and preserve the historic carousel, but they fell short of their fundraising goal before it was sold to an out-of-state purchaser in 2003. Undaunted, the society repurposed its mission to commission a new set of hand-carved, hand-painted carousel horses identical to the originals. In 2004 and 2005, the city of St. Joseph displayed the horses to bring awareness to the carousel fundraising efforts, and to entice visitors to downtown's shopping and eating venues. The display was marketed as "Horses on the Beach." That first public art exhibit was followed by "Beach Bears" in 2006, and "Hot Cars Cool Beaches" in 2007. Merchants also used the exhibits as a highly effective tool for merchandising and tourist attraction. The results were nothing short of spectacular. Foot traffic increased at virtually all times of day. By 2007, downtown business occupancy had swelled back to 93 percent.

In 2006, the Silver Beach Committee was formed to acquire the park property. But the property owners wisely refused to hand over the land until local leaders could agree on a sustainable plan for the field below the bluff that would truly enhance the community, both culturally and economically. Among the many proposals considered and discarded: a dog park, remote control boat launch, Silver Beach museum, train station museum, butterfly house, bocce ball courts, shuffle board courts, bell tower, parking lot, parking garage, condos, apartments, single family homes, row houses, open green space, sky tram, softball and baseball fields, retail spaces, winery, restaurant, botanical garden, coffee shop, elevated walkway, cooking school, and even a traffic circle.

Finally, all sides agreed on a concept with both seasonal and year-round facilities that would offer something for everyone: a carousel, a children's hands-on museum, a splash pad and fountain, a ballroom and events facility, concessions, and recreational beachfront. The new Silver Beach would provide recreational, cultural, and educational opportunities while celebrating the region's unique heritage. Just as importantly, it would operate as a financially stable enterprise that would not be a tax burden to the city's residents, but would instead be a legacy for future generations.

In an extraordinary example of public and private partnership, the city of St. Joseph, Whirlpool Corporation and Whirlpool Foundation, and several local families donated land and money to rebuild Silver Beach. The Silver Beach Carousel Society and the Curious Kids' Discovery Zone Museum were also essential participants in the project. Many "green" design features were included in the plans to facilitate grant opportunities, reduce operational costs, and preserve the environment.[1]

After more than two years of negotiations, planning, and fundraising, a groundbreaking was held on July 7, 2008, and the new facility was officially opened in late summer 2009.

Today, St. Joseph is once again a thriving city filled with color and life, with a healthy economy based on a balanced mixture of industry, commercial and residential development, and a booming tourist trade.

INVESTMENT

>> While it was clear that the city would have a piece of the project, they were not in a position to finance the whole thing, so public/private partnerships were essential to its success. In addition, one of the key decisions made early on was that this project had to be built without debt. Total project cost was $18 million. The city's share of that cost was $1.4 million. The vast majority of the funds came from the generosity of the

Whirlpool Corporation and Whirlpool Foundation, and a small group of local families who donated land and/or money. Over $8.2 million was raised to privately fund the project.

SOCIOECONOMIC IMPACT

>> An atmosphere of optimism and pride is evident throughout the downtown, where store owners are constantly touching up shop fronts and rearranging the details of their display windows for the steady flow of visitors strolling by.

>> Business went up 14 percent the year the Silver Beach Center opened, and has stayed up and gone even higher, said Janet Dykstra, owner of Kilwins of St. Joseph, a popular confectionary shop.

>> Boulevard Inn and Bistro general manager Christopher Heugel said revenue and occupancy have grown dramatically since the development opened.

As of 2013, the new Silver Beach Center has resulted in:
- 300 volunteers with 18,000 hours of service.
- 200 weddings in the Shadowland Ballroom.
- Over 600 community events in Shadowland Ballroom.
- 100,000+ visitors to the Curious Kids' Discovery Zone.
- Over 750,000 riders on the Silver Beach Carousel.

LESSONS LEARNED

>> Public art should be friendly, accessible, and interactive – At first, during "Horses on the Beach", they sought to protect the carousel horses with fences and "keep off" signs, which they later realized gave off the wrong message. In 2007, children were able to sit in the painted toy cars on display for "Hot Cars Cool Beaches".

>> Have clear goals and objectives – In the case of Silver Beach, the planners set priorities for financial sustainability, and a family-friendly recreation destination that would celebrate the city's heritage and offer something for everyone year-round. Completing the project without debt was also a high priority.

>> Be patient – It took several years for the city and its partners to come up with a development plan for Silver Beach that would achieve their stated goals. If they had rushed into development, they might have bowed to the pressures of one special interest group or another, and ended up with something of far less value and lasting impact.

>> Encourage and embrace public/private partnerships – Silver Beach Center would not have been possible without the generous and dedicated support and funding of the local business community, nonprofit foundations, and private citizens.

>> Get the word out – By partnering with residents and the local business community, St. Joseph has successfully developed a dynamic PR and marketing campaign.

(ENDNOTES)

1 "Silver Beach – St. Joseph, MI," Abonmarche, accessed April 24, 2014, http://www.abonmarche.com/Project.aspx?id=3.

Moving Placemaking Forward Through Waterfronts

• Community engagement is key, and the more frequent and well-informed the better, advises Marquette City Manager William Vajda. Conduct research and develop white papers identifying multiple visions based upon historic legacies and existing community plans (i.e. master plans, parks and recreation plans, arts and culture plans, sustainability plans, etc.). Use the white papers as a basis for dialogue in town hall meetings, local government work sessions, and one-on-one discussions. Also leverage the white papers to all media channels and services.

• Michigan Sea Grant's "Michigan Coastal Community Working Waterfronts Best Practices" is a how-to guide for waterfront redevelopment that can be applied to almost any community.[1] For example, the study recommends rezoning and subdividing former industrial property along the waterfront for mixed-use development – using a hybrid zoning ordinance that encourages mixed-use development, maintains connections and access to public spaces, and promotes walkability.